W9-BCY-262

NAVIGATING
through
MATHEMATICAL
CONNECTIONS
in
GRADES 6–8

David K. Pugalee
Fran Arbaugh
Jennifer M. Bay-Williams
Ann Farrell
Susann Mathews
David Royster

Susan N. Friel
Grades 6–8 Editor

Peggy A. House
Navigations Series Editor

NCTM®

NATIONAL COUNCIL OF
TEACHERS OF MATHEMATICS

Copyright © 2008 by
The National Council of Teachers of Mathematics, Inc.
1906 Association Drive, Reston, VA 20191-1502
(703) 620-9840; (800) 235-7566; www.nctm.org

All rights reserved

Navigating through mathematical connections in grades 6-8 / David K.
Pugalee ... [et al.].
    p. cm. — (Principles and standards for school mathematics
navigations series)
  Includes bibliographical references and index.
  ISBN 978-0-87353-593-9 (alk. paper)
  1. Mathematics—Study and teaching (Middle school)—Activity
programs--United States. 2. Problem solving--Study and teaching (Middle
school)—Activity programs—United States. I. Pugalee, David K.
QA13.N384 2008
510.71'2--dc22
                    2007047173

The National Council of Teachers of Mathematics is a public voice of mathematics education, providing vision, leadership, and professional development to support teachers in ensuring equitable mathematics learning of the highest quality for all students.

Permission to photocopy limited material from *Navigating through Mathematical Connections in Grades 6–8* is granted for educational purposes. On the CD-ROM, the blackline masters may be downloaded and reproduced for classroom distribution; the applets may be used for instructional purposes in one classroom at a time. For permission to photocopy material or use it electronically for all other purposes, please access www.copyright.com or contact the Copyright Clearance Center, Inc. (CCC), 222 Rosewood Drive, Danvers, MA 01923, 978-750-8400. CCC is a not-for-profit organization that provides licenses and registration for a variety of users. Permission does not automatically extend to any items identified as reprinted by permission of other publishers and copyright holders. Such items must be excluded unless separate permissions are obtained. It will be the responsibility of the user to identify such materials and obtain the permissions.

The publications of the National Council of Teachers of Mathematics present a variety of viewpoints. The views expressed or implied in this publication, unless otherwise noted, should not be interpreted as official positions of the Council.

Printed in the United States of America

APR 21 2010

NAVIGATIONS SERIES

TABLE OF CONTENTS

ABOUT THIS BOOK vii

INTRODUCTION 1

CHAPTER 1
Making Connections within Mathematics 7
  Ritzville Experiments 9

CHAPTER 2
Making Connections between Mathematics and Other Disciplines 39
  How Does the Shuttle Shape Up? 42
  Marvels of Flight 48
  Dinosaurs and Scaling 54
  The *Holes* Difference.. 59
  Fingerprinting Lab 70
  Who Committed the Crime? 79
  How Many Fish in the Pond? 88

LOOKING BACK AND LOOKING AHEAD 99

APPENDIX
Blackline Masters and Solutions................................... 101
  Pyramid Scheme? 102
  Ritzville Reflections 104
  Sizing Up a Cylinder 105
  Conic Considerations 107
  Completing the Circle 109
  Developing the Data 111
  Coming to the Surface 113
  Volumes Yet to Learn! 115
  Can You Be More Precise? 116
  Turning Up the Volume 120
  A Second Look at Cylinders 122
  A Value for the Volume 125
  Shuttle Silhouette 127
  Sizing the Silhouette 128
  Dinosaur Scaling 129
  Digging *Holes* 131
  Getting the *Holes* Picture 133
  Collecting Fingerprints 135
  Fingerprint Patterns 136
  Fingerprinting Lab 139
  My Binary-Coded Print 140
  Who Committed the Crime? 142
  Fishing for Data 145
  Reeling In an Estimate 147

Solutions for the Blackline Masters 150

REFERENCES 167

CONTENTS OF THE CD-ROM

Introduction

Table of Standards and Expectations, Process Standards, Pre-K–Grade 12

Applets

Areas of Irregular Polygons
Changing Slope and *y*-Intercept

Excel and Fathom Files for Ritzville Experiments

Volume of a Cone

Blackline Masters and Templates

All blacklines listed above plus the following:
Disk for "Completing the Circle"
Centimeter Grid Paper
Millimeter Grid Paper
Decimeter Grid Paper
Inch Grid Paper
A Cone and Its Net (transparency)
A Sector and Its Circle (transparency)
The Surface Area of a Cone
Basic and Composite Galton Characteristics

Readings from Publications of the National Council of Teachers of Mathematics

Building Properly Structured Mental Models for Reasoning
about Volume
Michael Battista
ON-Math

Exploring Proportional Reasoning through Movies and Literature
Charlene E. Beckmann, Denisse R. Thompson, and Richard A. Austin
Mathematics Teaching in the Middle School

Perimeter and Area of Similar Figures
Mary C. Enderson
Classroom Activities for "Learning and Teaching Measurement"

By the Unit or Square Unit
Bellasanta B. Ferrer, Bobbie Hunter, Kathryn C. Irwin,
Maureen J. Sheldon, Charles S. Thompson, and Catherine P.
Vistro-Yu
Mathematics Teaching in the Middle School

Other Ways to Count
Micah Fogel, ed.
Student Math Notes

Modeling Soft-Drink Packaging
  Gary Froelich
  Mathematics Teacher

Measuring the Mountain State
  Ted Hodgson
  Classroom Activities for "Learning and Teaching Measurement"

Flower Power: Creating an Engaging Modeling Problem to Motivate
Mathematics Students at an Alternative School
  Karen Koellner-Clark and Janice Newton
  Mathematics Teacher

Using Literature to Engage Students in Proportional Reasoning
  Sherri L. Martinie and Jennifer M. Bay-Williams
  Mathematics Teaching in the Middle School

Understanding Student Responses to Open-Ended Tasks
  Barbara M. Moskal
  Mathematics Teaching in the Middle School

Practical Geometry Problems: The Case of the Ritzville Pyramids
  Donald Nowlin
  Mathematics Teacher

Creating Rabbit Pens
  Margaret S. Smith and Melissa Boston
  Classroom Activities for "Learning and Teaching Measurement"

Let's Go Home
  Terry Souhrada, ed.
  Student Math Notes

Improving Middle School Teachers' Reasoning about Proportional Reasoning
  Charles S. Thompson and William S. Bush
  Mathematics Teaching in the Middle School

Improper Applications of Proportional Reasoning
  Wim Van Dooren, Dirk De Bock, Lieven Verschaffel, and Dirk Janssens
  Mathematics Teaching in the Middle School

Census 2000 and Sampling
  Sheryl Yamada, ed.
  Student Math Notes

Essay

Using Radian Measure to Investigate the Volume of a Cone
  David K. Pugalee, Fran Arbaugh, Jennifer M. Bay-Williams, Ann Farrell,
  Susann Mathews, and David Royster

About This Book

Making connections in mathematics is a complex process of understanding and appreciating the interrelatedness of diverse topics and their applications to the everyday world and other academic disciplines. This process fosters mathematical thinking that equips students to engage meaningfully in mathematics both inside and outside the classroom. Recognizing relationships promotes sense making, allowing students to find meaning in the world around them. Students who develop a broad awareness of the connections in mathematics can link conceptual and procedural knowledge—an achievement that prepares them to use mathematics in other curricular areas as well as their daily lives. As a result of viewing mathematics as an integrated whole, such students can—

- apply mathematical thinking and modeling to solve problems;
- use and value connections among mathematical topics at their full worth; and
- recognize equivalent representations of the same concept in different contexts (Coxford 1995).

Too often, students experience mathematics as a set of unrelated topics that also appear to be isolated from the other subjects that they study in school. In fact, students' experiences with mathematics often involve consideration of procedures and problems that lack any broad context, either inside or outside mathematics.

How can teachers facilitate students' understanding of mathematical connections in a way that not only enhances students' appreciation of the nature of mathematics but also increases their ability to recognize and make mathematical connections themselves? The activities and discussions in this book address this and related questions.

Attention to connections should be an integral part of any mathematics curriculum. The National Council of Teachers of Mathematics recognizes this fact in its Curriculum Principle (NCTM 2000): "A curriculum is more than a collection of activities; it must be coherent, focused on important mathematics, and well articulated across the grades" (p. 14). A coherent curriculum is one that demonstrates links and uses them to build students' learning experiences in such a way that the students' "understanding and knowledge deepens and their ability to apply mathematics expands" (NCTM 2000, p. 14).

NCTM continues to stress the need for a connected curriculum in *Curriculum Focal Points for Prekindergarten through Grade 8 Mathematics: A Quest for Coherence* (NCTM 2006). Instruction that incorporates communication, reasoning, representation, connections, and problem solving—the processes of "doing" mathematics—"can provide students with a connected, coherent, ever expanding body of mathematical knowledge and ways of thinking" (NCTM 2006, p. 1).

Adolescents typically look for patterns as they struggle to interpret the world around them. Young adolescents especially benefit from understanding the "big ideas" that guide and shape their learning. It is important for middle-grades students to engage in investigations that

"Thinking mathematically involves looking for connections, and making connections builds mathematical understanding."
(NCTM 2000, p. 274)

"A curriculum is more than a collection of activities; it must be coherent, focused on important mathematics, and well articulated across the grades."
(NCTM 2000, p. 14)

Many of the activities in this book also support core topics identified for emphasis in NCTM's *Curriculum Focal Points for Prekindergarten through Grade 8 Mathematics: A Quest for Coherence* (2006). This publication specifies by grade level essential content and processes that *Principles and Standards for School Mathematics* (NCTM 2000) discusses in depth by grade band.

"Without connections, students must learn and remember too many isolated concepts and skills. With connections, they can build new understandings on previous knowledge."
(NCTM 2000, p. 274)

help them see relationships between the mathematical ideas that they are currently studying and those that they have studied in the past. Recognizing these links enables them to appreciate how basic ideas continue to gain meaning and play significant roles in the new mathematics that they encounter in their studies. In addition, middle-grades students should engage in explorations that underscore the connections between mathematical inquiry and other subjects as well as the world around them. These explorations will provide students with flexible, thoroughly grounded thinking and reasoning skills.

The Organization of the Book

Navigating through Mathematical Connections in Grades 6–8 consists of two chapters, both of which emphasize the forging of connections as an important and essential outcome of middle-grade students' mathematical experiences. Both chapters present activities that contextualize important mathematical ideas and show their links to other areas of mathematics, other disciplines, and other real-world contexts. The activities help students model a variety of contexts mathematically, enabling them to discover relationships while gaining a sense of the broad usefulness of mathematics itself.

Behind all the activities are the expectations of the Connections Standard. This important Standard urges teachers to ensure that all instruction helps students "recognize and use connections among mathematical ideas," enables them to see how ideas "interconnect and build on one another" in a coherent whole, and gives meaning to "contexts outside mathematics" (NCTM 2000, p. 402).

Chapter 1 focuses on making connections within mathematics. A twelve-part activity based on the Ritzville "pyramids" (Nowlin 1993)—enormous stacks of wheat stored in Ritzville, Washington—engages students in investigating ideas from algebra, geometry, number, data analysis, and measurement. The experiments that the students undertake focus their attention on ideas and skills that are central to the middle school mathematics curriculum. The students use proportional reasoning, develop and apply formulas, and work with nets while developing important skills of spatial visualization. They apply appropriate tools and techniques for measuring and approximating. They collect, display, and analyze data. As they construct models to answer questions about surface area and volume, they have opportunities to experience how mathematical ideas and concepts grow, unfold, and are interrelated. The exploration shows them that a particular mathematical concept can arise in, and give meaning to, diverse topics in mathematics.

Chapter 2 presents a series of shorter, self-contained activities that demonstrate ways of helping students make connections between mathematics and other areas of experience. These activities can increase your students' appreciation of the influence of mathematics in the world around them. As your students make mathematical models in diverse real-world contexts, they will discover the powerful tools that mathematics offers for describing and interpreting phenomena and arriving at reasonable solutions to complex problems. The activities in chapter 2 engage the students in making mathematical connections to topics in literature, science, engineering, social studies, art, and other fields. The investigations illustrate the wide scope of the contexts, situations, and problems that mathematics can describe and explain.

Using the book

This book includes an accompanying CD-ROM that provides readings for teachers' professional development, supplemental investigations for students, and applets for learning experiences that promote students' awareness of connections. Teachers can allow students to use the applets in conjunction with particular activities or apart from them, to extend and deepen students' understanding. The resources on the CD support the central idea that "a comprehensive mathematics experience can prepare students for whatever career or professional path they may choose as well as equip them to solve many problems that they will face in the future" (NCTM 2006, p. 1). An icon in the margin (see the key) alerts readers to all materials on the CD.

Activity sheets for students appear as reproducible blackline masters in the appendix of the book, along with solutions to the problems. A second icon signals all blackline pages, which teachers can also print from the accompanying CD.

Throughout the book, margin notes supply teaching tips and pertinent ideas from *Principles and Standards for School Mathematics*. A third icon alerts the reader to these quotations, which highlight the fundamental notions that students should master the processes of mathematics and see mathematics as an integrated whole.

The authors of this book have not attempted to provide a complete curriculum for "connected mathematics." The activities offered here are intended to be illustrative rather than comprehensive, and students should encounter them in conjunction with other instructional materials in relevant contexts.

Key to Icons

Principles and Standards

CD-ROM

Blackline Master

Three different icons appear in the book, as shown in the key. One signals the blackline masters and indicates their locations in the appendix, another points readers to supplementary materials on the CD-ROM that accompanies the book, and a third alerts readers to material quoted from *Principles and Standards for School Mathematics*.

 "As students' knowledge of mathematics, their ability to use a wide range of mathematical representations, and their access to sophisticated technology and software increase, the connections they make with other academic disciplines … give them greater mathematical power." *(NCTM 2000, p. 354)*

NAVIGATIONS SERIES

GRADES 6–8

NAVIGATING *through* MATHEMATICAL CONNECTIONS

Introduction

Connections are at the heart of learning mathematics with understanding. The Learning Principle articulated in *Principles and Standards for School Mathematics* (NCTM 2000) stresses that "students' understanding of mathematical ideas can be built throughout their school years if they actively engage in tasks and experiences designed to deepen and connect their knowledge" (page 21). One result of such understanding is a readiness on the part of students to solve problems in a variety of settings.

Helping Middle-Grades Students Make Connections

The goal of this book is to share some ideas for helping middle-grades students make connections that will give them the mathematical readiness to think about and solve problems. The book's premise is that activities that engage students in mathematical modeling can promote their discovery of connections and their confidence in themselves as problem solvers.

A brief discussion of *mathematical modeling* can shed light on the indispensable support that modeling gives the Connections Standard. The term *mathematical modeling* has gained popularity and is often applied loosely to any problem-solving activity. However, problem solving and modeling are not identical activities. Although problem solving is at the heart of all mathematical modeling, modeling is not essential to all problem solving.

"A comprehensive mathematics experience can prepare students for whatever career or professional path they may choose as well as equip them to solve many problems that they will face in the future."
(NCTM 2006, p. 1)

1

Mathematical modeling is the use of mathematics to describe an actual phenomenon or event. Modeling is a powerful tool because the resulting mathematical description may be helpful in solving other, related problems based on real-world events. Froelich (2000) summarizes the problem-solving path that mathematical modeling typically takes as "the process of describing real-world phenomena in mathematical terms, obtaining mathematical results from the description, [and] then interpreting and evaluating the mathematical results in the real-world situation" (p. 478).

The activities in this book illustrate these ideas as well as the belief that helping students develop an understanding of mathematical modeling and skills for effective modeling requires that the students make conceptual connections—not only between mathematics and real-world phenomena but also among "big ideas" in mathematics. Figure 0.1 summarizes the steps in the process of mathematical modeling.

Fig. **0.1**.
The process of mathematical modeling

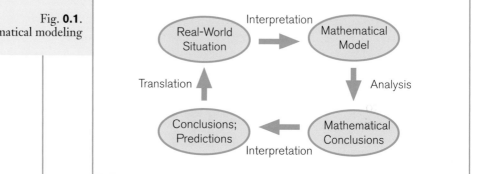

The modeling process begins with the identification of a problem arising in the context of a real-world phenomenon. It continues with the identification of the relevant mathematical factors in the situation and the expression of these factors in mathematical terms. In turn, this mathematical representation, or *model*, allows problem solvers to obtain mathematical results. Next, an analysis of these results in relation to the phenomenon under consideration enables the problem solvers to draw relevant conclusions or predictions about the real-world situation.

Garfunkel, Godbold, and Pollak (2000) discuss the use of this process to solve a problem arising in the lumber industry: A timber company wants to maximize the sustainable yield of lumber for each acre of timber. How does the company do this? Solving this problem calls for developing a model that identifies the best age for harvesting trees and predicts the amount of marketable lumber that any given tree yields, on the basis of its size or volume. Thus, the company needs a quick and efficient way to determine the volume of a tree from particular measurements. The company could use a measurement of the tree's diameter at the base or at a specified height to develop a model that would give a good estimate of the volume of the tree as a function of the measurement of this dimension. Once the company has a model, data can be selected to test the model and verify its appropriateness. The company would make refinements if the model failed to produce anticipated results with reasonable accuracy.

Activities such as this one support the three expectations of NCTM's Connections Standard, which states that "instructional programs from prekindergarten through grade 12 should enable all students to—

Froelich (2000; available on the CD-ROM) describes mathematical modeling and offers a modeling activity that lets students investigate ways of improving the efficiency of soft-drink packaging.

- recognize and use connections among mathematical ideas;
- understand how mathematical ideas interconnect and build on one another to produce a coherent whole;
- recognize and apply mathematics in contexts outside of mathematics" (NCTM 2000, p. 64).

The following sections consider each of these expectations in turn, setting each in the context of mathematics instruction for students in grades 6–8.

Students Should "Recognize and Use Connections among Mathematical Ideas"

Mathematical modeling is a process of investigating a problem to discern a mathematical core that provides information about the problem (Garfunkel, Godbold, and Pollak 2000). This mathematical core may merge ideas from several realms of mathematics, including number, geometry, algebra, data analysis, and measurement. Activities that connect multiple mathematical concepts can help students see relationships that transport them beyond a view of mathematics as a collection of unrelated concepts and skills. You can use modeling experiences to make these connections explicit to your middle-grades students.

For example, investigations of length-area relationships can help students make rich connections among mathematical ideas. Teachers often ask middle-grades students to investigate problems that involve them in establishing a maximum area or volume under certain constraints. In one common modeling activity, for instance, students investigate how to maximize the area that a given length of fencing can enclose. Investigating the problem requires the students to understand basic geometric concepts relating to area and perimeter. The collection of data and the development of a model require work with multiple representations, such as graphs and symbols. These representations reinforce the students' understanding of geometric properties, and teachers can use the representations to develop their students' thinking about domain, range, maximum and minimum values of a function, and limits (Day 1995).

See the discussion "Contrasting Linear Relationships with Other Kinds of Relationships" in *Navigating through Algebra in Grades 6–8* (Friel, Rachlin, and Doyle 2001, pp. 52–55) and the activity "Minimizing Perimeter" in *Navigating through Geometry in Grades 6–8* (Pugalee et al. 2002, pp. 73–76) for ideas related to length-area functions.

Students Should "Understand How Mathematical Ideas Interconnect and Build on One Another to Produce a Coherent Whole"

When students lack a strong conceptual understanding, they tend to view mathematics as a set of arbitrary rules. To overcome this tendency, students need experiences that involve them directly in connecting mathematical processes with mathematical concepts. As students progress through school, their work in mathematics should strengthen their abilities to see how similar ideas build on one another and how mathematical constructs apply in different settings.

For example, *equivalence* is a major mathematical concept that acquires more and more meaning as students advance through the mathematics curriculum. Children begin to develop a concept of equivalence in the early years as they explore numeric expressions, shapes, and

To help your students develop their understanding of the properties of equivalence, let them work with the activities on the Illuminations Web site at http://illuminations.nctm.org/LessonDetail.aspx?ID=U155.

symbolic expressions. In elementary school, they encounter the equals sign, which they may at first think of simply as a signal to perform an operation, such as addition or subtraction. However, their understanding should quickly extend to the equivalence of the quantities on either side of the sign. In other words, they should soon begin to understand that equivalence is a *relationship*—not an operation.

Students' concepts of equivalence deepen when they explore the equivalence of numerical representations and geometric objects, and their ideas expand again when they move to mathematical justifications and proofs. An understanding of equivalence is central to the development of algebraic thinking and plays a major role in skill in mathematical modeling. Students need many experiences with relationships involving quantities before they begin to grasp equivalence in more abstract contexts dealing with variables and symbolic expressions.

Students Should "Recognize and Apply Mathematics in Contexts Outside of Mathematics"

It is important for students to appreciate how mathematics shapes the world around us. Mathematical modeling gives life to the study of mathematics by enabling problem solvers to develop dynamic mathematical descriptions of events. These descriptions are powerful demonstrations of the role of mathematics in daily experiences and real-world phenomena. Focusing on the applications of mathematics provides opportunities for teaching mathematical concepts that students will need in the workplace and a host of other contexts throughout their lives.

Mathematical modeling activities in middle school should build on mathematical explorations that the students undertook in elementary school. Elementary school mathematics provides numerous opportunities for students to make conjectures or predictions related to real-world events. Students in grades 3–5 are beginning to formulate mathematical descriptions of events that will provide the necessary foundation for increasingly advanced experiences with modeling in grades 6–8.

For example, elementary students frequently study weather patterns, collect data, and make predictions on the basis of their observations. Consider the processes involved when students describe how to predict the best week in the summer for an outdoor camping trip. The development of the students' abilities to reason about relationships is essential to their understanding of how multiple variables interact. Experiences such as this can lay a foundation on which the students can construct mathematical models that capture the complexity of events. Such building blocks are necessary if middle-grades students are to deal with increasingly complex systems that require more and more abstraction and symbolic representation.

Mathematical Modeling and the Teacher

As a teacher of middle school mathematics, you undoubtedly watch vigilantly for opportunities to engage your students in explorations that will foster the development of their ideas about mathematics. Modeling problems provide multiple entry points for learners at various levels, enabling all learners to engage in meaningful mathematics. Although you cannot convert all problems into modeling tasks, some guidelines may assist you in identifying or adapting problems for modeling. Koellner-Clark and Newton (2003) offer the following tips:

- A modeling problem should encourage the development of a model that sufficiently answers the question posed. This model should be based on prior knowledge and should incorporate a sufficient degree of mathematical depth.
- The context of the problem should be realistic and should tie into students' prior knowledge and experiences.
- The model or derived solution should be useful for others in similar situations and should be assessable to the extent that students can determine whether their answers are appropriate and realistic.
- Products and models are actually processes, such that students' mathematical thinking of the concept or idea is usually transparent.
- The solution can be used as a general model for solving similar problems. (p. 430)

Koellner-Clark and Newton developed the modeling problem shown in figure 0.2.

 Koellner-Clark and Newton (2003; available on the CD-ROM) describe a modeling problem that motivated high school students to consider multiple solutions, real-life connections, and the usefulness of mathematics.

Fig. **0.2.**

Koellner-Clark and Newton's (2003) formulation of a real-world problem for students to solve by mathematical modeling

The Flower Power Problem

The football team at your high school wants to hire a group to make all the flowers for its float in the school parade. Your service club is interested in this project. The football team is taking bids for the job, and the job will go to the lowest bidder. The work must be done to the team's satisfaction and with quality materials.

For the float, the team wants to cover chicken wire with carnations made as described [at the right]. The area to be covered is 126 square feet. Two-ply Kleenex tissues cost $1.19 for a box of 100 tissues. A package of 100 pipe cleaners costs $2.00.

Your club has twenty members. If you get the bid, you will have a month to work on the project. Some of the members of the club can work on the project after school, but no one can work past 9:00 p.m. on school nights. None of the club members can start work until 4:00 p.m. on school days. No one will work on Friday nights, but some will work on Saturday nights. Everyone agrees to work whenever necessary on Saturday and any time on Sunday from noon until 9:00 p.m. Ten students can work on any weekday afternoon, and five can work on Saturday evenings. All twenty will work from 9:00 a.m. until 5:00 p.m. on Saturdays and from noon until 9:00 p.m. on Sundays, but no one will work for longer than six hours on any given day. You have four weeks and three weekends to do the project. You can hire additional students to work for $7.00 an hour.

With your group, determine whether the club can do the project and what your bid should be. You want to put in as low a bid as possible, but the club wants to make enough to pay its expenses (materials, $5.00 an hour for members' time, and $7.00 an hour for any outside helpers who might work) and to earn a small profit. Of course, the members will donate their time, so their wage figured into the bid is actually money made for the club.

You can use stopwatches, as well as graph paper and calculators.

You get a letter from your friend in another town. Her club is thinking of taking on the job of washing windows for the school. She is unsure how to determine what their price should be and whether the club should do the job. Write a letter to your friend, explaining how your club arrived at conclusions regarding the flower project.

How to Make the Flower

Use two 2-ply Kleenex tissues for each flower. Fit the two tissues on top of each other precisely and fold the two together lengthwise.

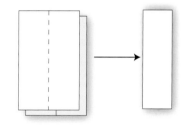

Take the folded tissues and fold back and forth from bottom to top, in an accordian pleat.

Now cut small notches on either side at the center and cut ends in a zig-zag (see below).

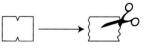

Then tightly twist a pipe cleaner over and around the center. Carefully pull the layers of tissue apart to make petals.

Teachers can modify many problems to provide mathematical modeling explorations. These problems may lead to short investigations or long ones, depending on the complexity of the problem. It is important to remember that problems that invite modeling involve students in applying multiple mathematical concepts and processes. Therefore, these problems have the potential to address several mathematics learning goals and objectives at once, while allowing students to develop and deepen their understanding of multiple ideas. Because modeling activities have rich applications in mathematics, they hold the potential to engage students more actively in thinking about important ideas than do conventional problems requiring the use of procedures in purely numerical contexts.

Teaching mathematical modeling calls for important changes in classroom practice and approaches to problem solving. Research with elementary students has identified three aspects of conventional classroom problem solving that teachers need to modify to engage students successfully in solving context-based mathematics problems (Verschaffel et al. 2000).

First, the story problems that mathematics lessons typically present follow standard, predictable patterns, and their solutions tend to depend on computations that are straightforward. To overcome these shortcomings, teachers need to offer their students more problems that are nonstandard and embed complex and subtle relationships between mathematics and the physical world.

Second, to help students approach such problems, teachers must use powerful interactive techniques and processes. These include modeling, coaching, articulating, reflecting, exploring, and "scaffolding"—that is, erecting a structure for learning that allows students to climb with maximum independence from the level that they have mastered to the next level that they are capable of attaining. Mathematical modeling activities invite these kinds of techniques and processes, all of which have the potential to foster heuristic and metacognitive skills.

Third, the classroom culture must move away from traditional classroom rituals and practices that reinforce fragmented views of mathematics. These practices include encouraging students to apply prescribed solution strategies more or less mindlessly to given problems.

Mathematical modeling offers a very powerful and effective response to all these concerns. This book provides some ideas, strategies, and activities that can help you implement such practices, empowering you to guide your students to the kinds of robust mathematical learning experiences that can make them flexible, versatile problem solvers. Moreover, such experiences are essential to giving your students a sophisticated grasp of mathematics as a highly interconnected field, with a myriad of links to other areas of experience as well.

Heuristic skills enable people to make discoveries and learn for themselves. Mathematical modeling activities invite techniques and processes that have the potential to foster heuristic and metacognitive skills.

NAVIGATIONS SERIES

GRADES 6–8

NAVIGATING *through* MATHEMATICAL CONNECTIONS

Chapter 1
Making Connections within Mathematics

It is particularly important that instruction in middle school focus students' attention on making mathematical connections. The middle grades are a crucial time for students to develop a disposition to draw on such connections rather than to approach problems with a set of disjointed mathematical facts and skills.

Helping Students Build Mathematical Ideas on One Another

Research has found that when high- and low-achieving students encounter tasks in geometry, differences in their success depend more on the connectedness of a student's knowledge than on "what problem-relevant knowledge is available to the student" (Lawson and Chinnappan 2000, p. 41). As students use connections that they have learned or discovered on their own, new ideas become extensions of mathematics that they have already encountered. "If curriculum and instruction focus on mathematics as a discipline of connected ideas, students learn to expect mathematical ideas to be related" (NCTM 2000, p. 275).

Substantive mathematical problems—problems set in real-world contexts—encourage students to consider ways of applying familiar concepts and skills to new situations. Such problems help students see

"If curriculum and instruction focus on mathematics as a discipline of connected ideas, students learn to expect mathematical ideas to be related."

(NCTM 2000, p. 275)

connections and develop new understanding. "In classrooms where students are expected to reason mathematically and to communicate clearly about significant mathematical tasks, new ideas surface quite naturally as extensions of previously learned mathematics" (NCTM 2000, p. 275).

As a middle school mathematics teacher, you face the challenge of helping your students develop their understanding of the connections among the topics and ideas that they encounter. This challenge begins with the task of choosing problems in which new mathematics flows naturally from the mathematics that your students already understand. Once you have your students working toward solutions on such problems, you can encourage them to look for connections by posing such questions as—

- "Is this problem similar to any other problem that you have previously solved?"
- "How is it similar?"
- "How is it different?"

Later, you can revisit the problem to connect the ideas that your students have discovered with new concepts and skills. In this way, you can assist them in developing their knowledge of mathematics as a unified whole instead of a collection of isolated topics.

Students arriving in middle school should have had many previous opportunities to build and draw three-dimensional figures, analyze attributes of two- and three-dimensional objects, use different representations to model problem situations, estimate areas and volumes of objects, and apply appropriate tools to measure lengths, areas, and volumes (NCTM 2000, pp. 164, 170). Instruction in middle school deepens these ideas.

Chapter 1 presents a twelve-part activity, Ritzville Experiments, which can facilitate this process while helping students make connections among ideas from the middle-grades curricula for algebra, geometry, number, data analysis, and measurement. In addition, the various parts of the activity and their accompanying blackline pages offer multiple entry and exit points to allow students at different levels and with different experiences to examine the problems in different ways.

To solve the problems, the students apply proportional reasoning, develop and use formulas, work with two-dimensional nets of three-dimensional objects, and visualize objects in a three-dimensional space. They also display data, learn to apply appropriate tools and techniques for measuring and approximating, and build a foundation for the concepts of a limit and maximization. The discussion of the exploration reflects the work of teachers and students in several actual middle-grades mathematics classes.

"The acquisition of mathematical concepts and procedures means little if the content is learned in an isolated way in which connections among the various mathematical topics are neglected.... Connections ... [can] influence students' beliefs about the value of mathematics in society and its contributions to other disciplines."

(NCTM 1991, pp. 89–90)

Ritzville Experiments

Goals

Students investigate a real-world problem to—

- apply ideas and skills from multiple strands of mathematics, including algebra, geometry, number, measurement, and data analysis;
- extend their facility with proportional reasoning;
- develop and use formulas;
- work with nets of solids and visualize objects in three-dimensional space;
- use appropriate tools and techniques for measuring and approximating;
- build foundations for the concepts of maximization and limit.

Materials and Equipment

Part 1—"Pyramid Scheme?"

For each student—

- A copy of the blackline master "Pyramid Scheme?"

For each group of three students—
- Three 1-cup containers of rice
- A small, fairly flat pan (pizza pan or pie pan, for example)
- A paper towel

Part 2—"Ritzville Reflections"

For each student—

- A copy of the blackline master "Ritzville Reflections"

Part 3—"Sizing Up a Cylinder"

For each student—

- A copy of the blackline master "Sizing Up a Cylinder"

For each group of three students—

- A cylindrical object, such as a cardboard paper-towel core or a soup can with the label attached
- A pair of scissors
- A piece of cream-colored cardstock or a sheet of unlined white paper
- A roll of transparent tape
- Three colored pens or pencils, in different colors

For the teacher—

- A small assortment of empty cardboard boxes (from dry cereal, candy, reams of paper, etc.) to break down to demonstrate nets
- A small set of Polydrons (flat plastic pieces that interlock to form polyhedra)

This activity is adapted from Nowlin (1993).

Donald Nowlin's article "Practical Geometry Problems: The Case of the Ritzville Pyramids" (1993), which provides the basis for the exploration Ritzville Experiments, is available on the accompanying CD-ROM.

pp. 102–3

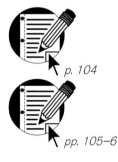

p. 104

pp. 105–6

Polydron Pieces

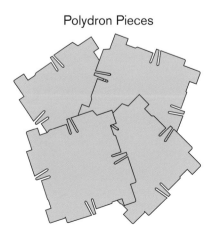

pp. 107–8

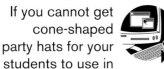

If you cannot get cone-shaped party hats for your students to use in part 4 ("Conic Considerations"), you can make usable, smaller hats with the template "Disk for 'Completing the Circle'" on the CD-ROM.

pp. 109–10

Part 4—"Conic Considerations"

For each student—

- A copy of the blackline master "Conic Considerations"

For each group of three students—

- A conical party hat
- A pair of scissors
- A piece of cream-colored cardstock or a sheet of unlined white paper
- A roll of transparent tape
- Four pens or pencils in different colors (can be the three colors from part 3 plus one more or entirely different colors)

For the teacher—

- An overhead projector (optional)
- A transparency of "A Cone and Its Net" (optional blackline; available on the CD-ROM)

Part 5—"Completing the Circle"

For each student—

- A copy of the blackline master "Completing the Circle"

For each pair of students—

- Two flexible, fairly flat paper plates, or two disks on cardstock or paper, made from the template "Disk for 'Completing the Circle'" (available on the CD-ROM)
- A protractor
- A straightedge

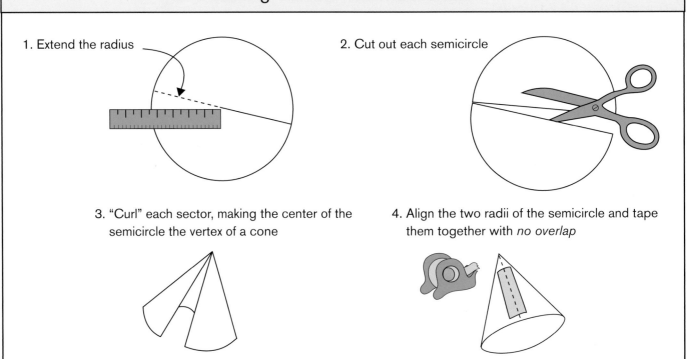

Making Conical Hats from a Disk

1. Extend the radius

2. Cut out each semicircle

3. "Curl" each sector, making the center of the semicircle the vertex of a cone

4. Align the two radii of the semicircle and tape them together with *no overlap*

- A pair of scissors
- A thin string (about one meter long)
- Two or three sheets of centimeter grid paper (template available on the CD-ROM)
- Two or three sheets of decimeter grid paper (optional; template on the CD-ROM)
- Two or three sheets of millimeter grid paper (optional; template on the CD-ROM)
- A calculator (optional)
- A roll of transparent tape (optional)

For the teacher—
- An overhead projector (optional)
- A transparency of "A Sector and Its Circle" (optional blackline; available on the CD-ROM)

If paper plates are unavailable for part 5 ("Completing the Circle"), you can make suitable disks by reproducing the template "Disk for 'Completing the Circle'" (on the CD-ROM) on cardstock or unlined paper. The CD also includes the templates "Centimeter Grid Paper," "Millimeter Grid Paper" and "Decimeter Grid Paper" for students' use in this and other parts of the exploration.

Part 6—"Developing the Data"
For each student—
- A copy of the blackline master "Developing the Data"
- A sheet of centimeter grid paper (template available on the CD-ROM)

For each pair of students (same pairs as in part 5, if possible)—
- A calculator

pp. 111–12

Part 7—"Coming to the Surface"
For each student—
- A copy of the blackline master "Coming to the Surface"
- A calculator
- A copy of "The Surface Area of a Cone" (optional blacklines; available on the CD-ROM)

For the teacher—
- An overhead projector (optional)
- Transparencies of "The Surface Area of a Cone" (optional blacklines; available on the CD-ROM)

pp. 113–14

Part 8—"Volumes Yet to Learn!"
For each student—
- A copy of the blackline master "Volumes Yet to Learn!"

Part 9—"Can You Be More Precise?"
For each student—
- A copy of the blackline master "Can You Be More Precise?"

For each pair of students (same pairs as in parts 5 and 6, if possible)—
- The two cones from part 5, *or* two cones made as in part 5
- Two to three cups of rice in a plastic tub (can reuse from part 1)
- A 10-milliliter graduated cylinder
- A 100-milliliter graduated cylinder

pp. 115

pp. 116–19

The unit "Exploring Geometric Solids and Their Properties" on NCTM's Illuminations Web site presents five lessons for grades 3–5 that help build a foundation for middle school. See http://illuminations .nctm.org/index_o.aspx?id=122.

pp. 120–21

pp. 122–24

pp. 125–26

A net is a two-dimensional pattern, or diagram in a plane, of a three-dimensional solid. The net can be folded to form the solid.

- Approximately 150 plastic centimeter cubes
- Approximately 20 plastic cubes that are 2 centimeters on an edge
- A piece of cardstock or a sheet of unlined paper
- A straightedge calibrated in centimeters
- A pair of scissors
- A roll of transparent tape

Part 10—*Turning Up the Volume*

For each student—
- A copy of the blackline master "Turning Up the Volume"
- One or two sheets of centimeter grid paper
- Three colored pens or pencils, in different colors

Part 11—*"A Second Look at Cylinders"*

For each student—
- A copy of the blackline master "A Second Look at Cylinders"
- One of the two cones that the student made with his or her partner in part 5 and reused in part 9
- Two or three sheets of centimeter grid paper
- A calculator

For the teacher—
- A copy of "Using Radian Measure to Investigate the Volume of a Cone" (optional; supplemental essay on the CD-ROM)

Part 12—*"A Value for the Volume"*

For each student—
- A copy of the blackline master "A Value for the Volume"
- A calculator

Learning Environment

The teacher presents a real-world context and guides the students' exploration of problems embedded in it, listening carefully to their discussions. The students frequently work together in pairs or groups of three, asking each other questions and conversing about the problems in an environment that helps them forge connections in their thinking. The blackline activity sheets prompt the students to approach the problems with mathematics that they already know and then to build on those ideas as they work. Discussions with one another and with the teacher make the connections explicit and help the students develop their mathematical vocabularies, thus increasing their capacity to participate in future discussions of mathematical ideas.

Prior Knowledge or Experience

The students should have explored the circumferences of circles; the areas of rectangles, triangles, and circles; and the surface areas, nets, and volumes of cylinders and some polyhedra. The students' understanding of geometric solids and their properties should include a vocabulary for identifying, comparing, and analyzing attributes of three-dimensional shapes. They should be able to describe and reason about transformations of two-dimensional nets into three-dimensional solids, and their skills in spatial visualization should enable them to recognize relationships among three-dimensional shapes and construct arguments about them.

Overview

Many farmers in the eastern part of the state of Washington store their surplus wheat at an expansive outdoor facility near a small town named Ritzville. The facility piles the wheat in very large vinyl-covered stacks, which passing motorists have called the "Ritzville pyramids." This real-world situation provides the context for a twelve-part exploration based on Nowlin's (1993) discussion of the wheat stacks in Ritzville and the related embedded mathematical problems.

In part 1 ("Pyramid Scheme?"), the students consider whether such a stack of wheat would actually form a *pyramid*. If not, what shape would the stack have? In this natural way, students begin a multipart exploration of cones. Hands-on work with rice shows the students that many grains of rice would fall into a cone-shaped stack, and they conclude that the same would be true of many grains of wheat.

Part 2 ("Ritzville Reflections") encourages the students to think about the elements of a cone as they begin to consider two problems embedded in the Ritzville context: (1) how much heavy-duty protective vinyl would it take to cover a conical pile of wheat with a slant height of 91 feet and a circumference of 482 feet? and (2) how much wheat would be in such a stack? At this stage, the students simply consider what measurements they would need to make to solve the problems; they attempt no calculations.

In part 3 ("Sizing Up a Cylinder"), the students begin to grapple with the problem about the area of the vinyl on the lateral surface of the Ritzville stack by thinking about a net. Before considering the net of a cone, however, they investigate the simpler net of a cylinder. The more experience your students have had with nets of polyhedra and cylinders, the more prepared they will be for visualizing the net of a cone.

Part 4 ("Conic Considerations") invites the students to transfer their discoveries about a cylinder to a cone. They examine the surface areas of cones by cutting conical party hats and inspecting the resulting nets. They discover that the net of the lateral surface of a cone is a sector of a circle.

In part 5 ("Completing the Circle"), the students apply their discovery from part 4. They move closer to calculating the area of a cone's lateral surface by cutting out sectors of a circle and comparing each sector's circumference or area with that of the whole circle. They practice measuring skills, use familiar formulas, and develop facility with proportional reasoning by considering the following claim:

$$\frac{\textit{Area of sector}}{\textit{Area of circle}} = \frac{\textit{Circumference of sector}}{\textit{Circumference of circle}}.$$

Part 6 ("Developing the Data") guides the students in collecting and analyzing data to substantiate the claim that they considered in part 5.

To give your students additional experience in constructing and analyzing polyhedra, their two-dimensional nets, and their cross sections, see the applet "Spinning and Slicing Polyhedra" and the template "Nets of Polyhedra" on the CD-ROM for *Navigating through Geometry in Grades 6–8* (Pugalee et al. 2002), as well as other related activities and blackline pages in that book.

A pointed party hat can give students a convenient visual example of a cone. However, in mathematics a cone has a circular base – it is not open like a party hat.

Part 5 gives students an opportunity to choose and "apply appropriate techniques … and formulas" (NCTM, 2000, p. 240) for measuring, as the Measurement Standard recommends.

The students' work in part 6 obviously supports the Data Analysis and Probability Standard, but it also supports the Algebra Standard, which calls for all students to "represent, analyze, and generalize a variety of patterns with tables, graphs, words, and when possible, symbolic rules" (NCTM 2000, p. 222).

They calculate the fraction of 360 degrees (a circle's central angle) that their sector's central angle represents, and they compare this ratio to the ratios in the claim. They use a chart to organize their data, a calculator to compute ratios, and words to explain their results. They discover that for a sector and its respective circle, all three ratios are equal:

$$\frac{(Central\ angle)_{sector}}{(Central\ angle)_{circle}} = \frac{(Circumference)_{sector}}{(Circumference)_{circle}} = \frac{(Area)_{sector}}{(Area)_{circle}}.$$

In part 7 ("Coming to the Surface"), the students apply their discoveries from part 6 to solve the first Ritzville problem: How many square feet of vinyl would it take to cover a stack of wheat with a slant height of 91 feet and a circumference of 482 feet? The students use representation; apply ideas from geometry, algebra, measurement, and data analysis; and experience firsthand the power of proportional reasoning in problem solving.

The students turn their attention to the second Ritzville problem in part 8 ("Volumes Yet to Learn!"). To find the amount of wheat in their Ritzville stack, they must now consider the *volume* of a cone rather than the area of its lateral surface.

To begin work on this problem, the students experiment with rice again in part 9 ("Can You Be More Precise?") Working with cones that have the same slant height but different heights and circumferences, they explore three measurement methods that give increasingly precise values for the volume of a cone. Their work gives them a hands-on experience in refining the precision of a measurement.

In part 10 ("Turning Up the Volume"), the students pool the data that they collected in part 9 and determine which cone has the greatest volume and what fraction of a whole circle someone removed to make it. This experience lays foundations for thinking about limits and maximizing—fundamental ideas of calculus. More immediately, the students explore relationships among circles, circular regions, and cones. They develop their understanding of geometry and their spatial sense, and they appreciate the value of collecting, displaying, and analyzing data.

Part 9 helps the students "understand, select, and use units of appropriate size and type," as the Measurement Standard recommends (NCTM 2000, p. 240).

In part 11 ("A Second Look at Cylinders"), the students focus on the volume of a cylinder. They select one of the cones whose volume they measured in part 9, and they compare its volume with that of a cylinder whose height and radius, respectively, are the same as the height of the cone and the radius of its base. They gather data from their classmates on other such paired cones and cylinders, and their analysis of their data allows them to reason inductively that the volume of a cone is one-third of the volume of the paired cylinder.

The students' experimental development of the formula for the volume of a cone in part 11 prepares them to bring their work on volume to a conclusion in part 12 ("A Value for the Volume"). By applying their discoveries about the volume of a cone, they can now easily solve the second Ritzville problem about the amount of wheat in a stack with a slant height of 91 feet and a circumference of 482 feet.

Discussion

You can implement the activity Ritzville Experiments with inquiry-based instruction, guiding your students to—

- engage;
- explore;
- explain;
- evaluate;
- elaborate, or extend.

As the students *engage* in examining the situation and its embedded mathematical problems, they make observations and pose questions. They move back and forth between *exploring* and *explaining* the interconnections that they find, and from time to time, they stop to analyze and *evaluate*. They *elaborate*, communicating their results, and possibly *extending* their ideas. They may need to reengage, beginning the cycle again.

Introduce the real-world situation that gives rise to the mathematical questions in Ritzville Experiments by giving each student a copy of the activity sheet for part 1, "Pyramid Scheme?" Read aloud the presentation of the Ritzville pyramids. Alternatively, you can ask for a student volunteer to read it, or you can have all the students read it for themselves:

> In the eastern part of the state of Washington, many farmers grow wheat. When they produce a surplus, they often store their unsold wheat in huge outdoor piles, which they cover with large pieces of heavy-duty vinyl to protect them from wind, snow, and rain. Motorists driving on Interstate 90 near the small community of Ritzville come on an immense storage area with many vinyl-covered stacks of wheat. Some travelers have described the enormous stacks rising from the rolling plains as "pyramids." In fact, the stacks have been called the "Ritzville pyramids."

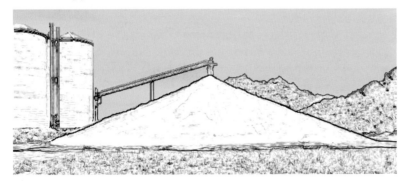

Engage the whole class in a brief discussion of the scene in Ritzville by posing questions like the following:

- "Have you ever seen piles of wheat like the stacks in Ritzville?"
- "Do you have any idea how high the piles might be?"

Part 1—"Pyramid Scheme?"

Set the students to work on the activity sheet for part 1, "Pyramid Scheme?" Direct them to work independently on step 1, which asks them to consider what a *pyramid* is. They must offer a definition and decide whether or not they think the Ritzville stacks of wheat would qualify as pyramids. If not, what shape would the students expect the stacks to have?

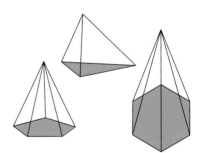

A pyramid is a polyhedron whose base is a polygon and whose faces are triangles that have a common vertex.

Next, the students explore their ideas by experimenting with rice. Assign them to groups of three for this work, and equip each group with a small flat pan, a paper towel, and three one-cup containers of rice. The students line the pan with the paper towel and pour the rice onto the towel *very slowly*, one cup at a time, forming a pile. They draw their pile of rice at different times and from different vantage points. They should see that their stacks are becoming cone-shaped. When they have completed the experiment, ask, "Can you give other examples of cones that occur outside the classroom?" The students are likely to suggest ice cream cones, traffic cones, volcanoes, and so on.

Emphasize to your students that they should pour their rice *very slowly*. As they work, they may at first think that their piles are simply mounds; however, if they continue to pour slowly and carefully, they should see that the rice is beginning to form cones.

One teacher who guided sixth graders through the experiment of pouring rice into piles found that having the students draw both "top" and "side" views of each three-dimensional figure that they created was a powerful way of helping them connect two-dimensional cross sections with three-dimensional shapes. The drawing exercise thus proved to be an excellent means of developing the students' three-dimensional spatial sense.

In general, middle-grades teachers who worked with the activity agreed that the time that their students devoted to pouring and drawing before they began working with the surface areas and volumes of the cones was very well spent. These activities proved to be very beneficial in helping students construct an understanding of three-dimensional shapes.

Part 2—"Ritzville Reflections"

Now persuaded that a large stack of wheat would be cone-shaped, the students are prepared to reengage with the Ritzville situation and its embedded mathematics. To focus their thinking, they now suppose that they are wheat farmers who have stored surplus wheat in a large vinyl-covered stack in the storage facility in Ritzville. They can easily measure the circumference, C, of the base of the stack by walking around it. In addition, because the vinyl covering stabilizes the stack, they can measure its *slant height, s.* The students suppose that they have measured *C* as 482 feet and *s* as 91 feet, making both measurements to the nearest foot.

Part 2 turns the students' attention to two problems at the heart of the real-world situation: (1) how much vinyl would the facility use in covering their stack? and (2) how much wheat is in the stack? (The students are told that they need to declare the amount for an inventory at the storage facility.) They make no calculations at this point; they merely identify the quantities that these questions ask them to measure—the *surface area* and *volume* of the cone formed by the stack of wheat. These reflections prepare them to explore the properties of a cone.

Part 3—"Sizing Up a Cylinder"

Part 3 launches an extensive consideration of the surface area of a cone as an approach to the first Ritzville problem—how much vinyl would it take to cover the stack of wheat discussed in part 2? The students' interaction with this problem continues through part 7 as they explore, explain, evaluate, and elaborate or extend their ideas.

Distribute copies of the blackline activity page "Sizing Up a Cylinder" to your students. The activity sheet introduces the idea of a *net*—a two-dimensional pattern for a three-dimensional solid—as an entry point to the first Ritzville problem.

If your students have not previously worked with nets of polyhedra, provide them with three-dimensional objects—cereal boxes and so on—that they can cut apart and unfold to acquaint themselves with nets. Solids made from plastic polyhedral pieces (available commercially) will also work well. After the students have made nets from three-dimensional shapes, reverse the process, giving them assorted two-dimensional shapes to fold into three-dimensional polyhedra.

After introducing the idea of a net, the activity sheet focuses on the net of a *cylinder*—a solid whose net is simpler than that of a cone. Farmers often store hay out in the open in large cylindrical rolls. Expand on this information if you wish, fleshing out a real-world context for cylinders that is related to the Ritzville context for cones.

As in part 1, assign your students to groups of three, this time to explore the net of a cylindrical object, such as the stiff core from a roll

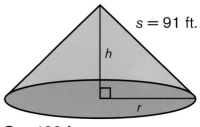

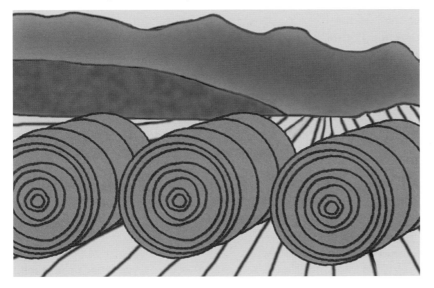

Going from two-dimensional shapes to three-dimensional figures and from three-dimensional figures to two-dimensional shapes provides experiences with connecting part to whole and whole to part.

The unit "Packages and Polygons" in *Mathematics in Context* (Kindt et al. 1998) offers helpful activities for exploring a variety of three-dimensional shapes (polyhedra and nonpolyhedra).

 The Cubes Applet in "Building Properly Structured Mental Models for Reasoning about Volume" (Battista 2002; available on the CD-ROM) can help your students visualize prisms and can assist you in assessing their understanding of the surface areas and volumes.

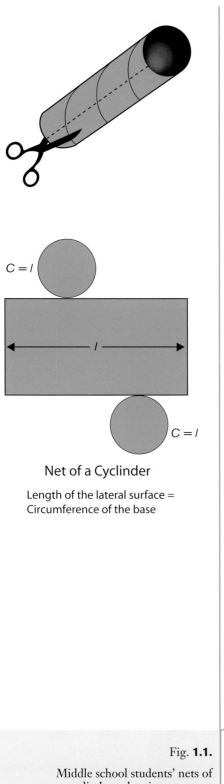

$C = l$

$\longleftarrow \quad l \quad \longrightarrow$

$C = l$

Net of a Cyclinder

Length of the lateral surface =
Circumference of the base

of paper towels or the label on a can of soup. After speculating about the likely shape of the net, the students experiment to check their ideas. They cut their cylinder from edge to edge, making the shortest possible cut (see the margin), and they discover that the net of the lateral surface of the cylinder is a rectangle.

The students consider that cylinders also have *bases*, and they discuss how they could make bases for their cylindrical object and where they would place them in its net. They continue to investigate these ideas by visualizing a different cylinder and completing three tasks in any order:

- They draw their new cylinder as viewed from the side.
- They construct a model of their new cylinder from cardstock or paper.
- They draw the net of their new cylinder.

Using a color code, they identify in each of the three items (*a*) the cylinder's lateral surface, (*b*) its bases, and (*c*) the circumferences of its bases. Their work should help them discover that they can place one of the cylinder's bases anywhere on the top edge of the net of its lateral surface, and the other one anywhere on the bottom edge.

In working with middle school students on this part of the activity, teachers found a common misconception—even among students who had spent time investigating nets of polyhedra before constructing nets of three-dimensional figures with curved surfaces, such as a cylinder. When drawing the net of a cylinder, including the two bases, the students routinely made the circles for the bases much too small. To counteract this tendency, you might have each group of students begin with a can with an affixed label. The students can remove the label to create the net of the lateral surface of the cylinder and then trace the base of the upright can on each of two parallel sides of the lateral surface to complete the net.

In one middle school classroom, a student noticed that the net that she and her partners had created on grid paper did not form a cylinder. She reported on the group's efforts to rectify the situation: "The rectangle was too long, so we cut off three rows." Figure 1.1a illustrates the group's work before cutting the rectangle down to size. (Note that by "rows," the student actually meant three columns of grid squares.)

Some other students in the classroom believed that they had to place the circular bases of the cylinder in the middle of the edges of the rectangular lateral surface in the net. Figure 1.1b illustrates this idea. In addition, the students who created this net ignored the relative sizes of the circumference of the bases and the side length of the lateral surface.

Fig. 1.1.

Middle school students' nets of cylinders, showing common misconceptions about the relationship between the size of the rectangle (representing the cylinder's lateral surface) and the size of the circles (representing the cylinder's bases)

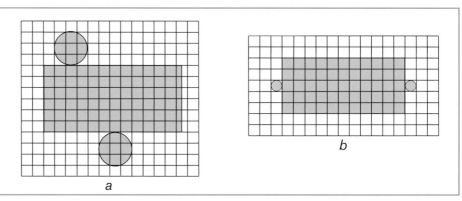

Navigating through Mathematical Connections in Grades 6–8

Part 4—"Conic Considerations"

Part 4 repeats the format of part 3, with cones now replacing cylinders as the focus. Show your students a conical party hat as a familiar, commonplace example of a cone without a base. Give each student a copy of the blackline master "Conic Considerations," and again divide the class into groups of three. Give each group a conical party hat.

As in part 3, the students speculate about the likely shape of the net before experimenting to check their ideas. They then cut their cone-shaped hat from brim to crown, making the shortest cut possible (see the illustration below) and flattening the hat to form the net of the lateral surface of a cone. Be sure that your students understand that the resulting net is a *sector of a circle*.

As an alternative to commercially manufactured party hats, you can make small cone-shaped hats from the template "Disk for 'Completing the Circle'" on the CD-ROM; see the instructions at the bottom of p. 10.

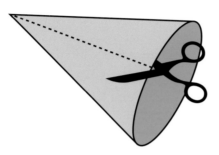

The students consider the fact that a cone, by definition, has a *base*; they discuss how they could make a base for their conical hat and where they would place it on the net. They then investigate their ideas by visualizing a different cone and completing three tasks as in part 3, again in any order:

- They draw their new cone as viewed from the side.
- They construct a model of their new cone from cardstock or paper.
- They draw the net of their new cone.

As before, they use color coding, this time identifying four elements in each of the three items: (*a*) the cone's lateral surface, (*b*) its slant height, (*c*) its base, and (*d*) the circumference of its base. Their work should help them discover that they can place the cone's base anywhere on the circumference of the sector that forms its lateral surface.

In some middle school classrooms, teachers observed that students who worked on this exploration often drew the net of a cone as a triangle and a circle. Typically, they made the diameter of the circle equal to the base of the triangle (see fig. 1.2a). Other students described the net of the lateral surface of the cone as "a triangle with a rounded bottom," which they drew as in figure 1.2b. This shape of course more nearly approaches the actual shape—a sector of a circle. The teachers also noted that in drawing nets of cones, middle school students were likely to encounter the same problem with the circle for the base that they encountered with circles for the bases of their cylinders. Once again, many students made their circles far too small. Having the students reshape the party hat as a cone and then trace around its base proved to be a very effective technique for giving the students a concrete sense of the actual size relationship between the two regions of the net.

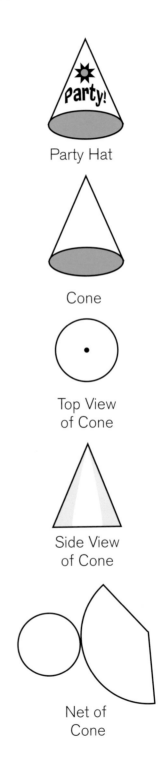

Party Hat

Cone

Top View
of Cone

Side View
of Cone

Net of
Cone

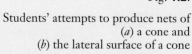

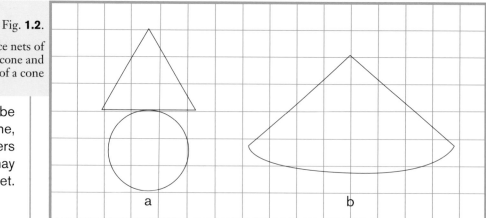

Fig. **1.2**.

Students' attempts to produce nets of
(*a*) a cone and
(*b*) the lateral surface of a cone

Eighth graders will probably be able to draw the net of a cone, but sixth and seventh graders may need assistance—you may even need to give them the net.

If a circle is cut into two sectors that are not congruent, the sectors will form the surface areas of two different cones: The cones have the same *slant height* (equal to the radius of the uncut circle) but differ in *height* and *circumference of the base*.

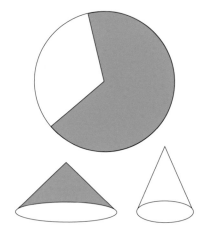

Depending on your overall sense of your students' work in part 4, you may want to reinforce or clarify their understanding of the connection between a cone and its net, as well as their vocabularies for discussing a cone, before moving on to part 5. You can use a transparency of the blackline master "A Cone and Its Net" (see the CD-ROM) with the whole class to be sure that your students understand the correspondence between the three-dimensional solid and its two-dimensional net as well as the relevant mathematical terms.

Part 5—"Completing the Circle"

The discovery in part 4 that the net of the lateral surface of a cone is a sector of a circle brings the students a big step closer to solving the first Ritzville problem about how much vinyl it would take to cover the stack of wheat. Introduce the exploration in part 5 with a brief discussion of the circumference and area of a circle, reviewing the relationships $C = 2\pi r$ and $A = \pi r^2$. Encourage your students to refer to their color-coded models and drawings from part 4 as they conjecture about the relationships (1) between the sector that forms the net of the lateral surface of the cone and the whole circle to which the sector belongs, and (2) between the cone's slant height and the radius of the whole circle.

The students' work from part 4 should make the relationship between the slant height and the radius fairly easy to recognize. The students can see that the cone's slant height is equal to the radius of the circle from which the cone's lateral surface was "cut." Relationships between the sector and the circle are less obvious, however, and become the focus of the students' work in part 5.

You might say to your students, "You have discovered how to make a net of a cone. Your net is a sector with an attached circle. The sector is part of a different full circle. How does the area of the sector compare with the area of that full circle? How does the circumference of the sector—just the curved edge—compare with the circumference of that full circle?"

Distribute copies of the blackline master "Completing the Circle" to each student, arrange the students in pairs, and give each pair two paper plates or other equal-sized disks. Inexpensive, flexible paper plates are easy to draw on and cut but are still sturdy enough to make serviceable cones. (If such paper plates are not available, use the template "Disk for

'Completing the Circle'" on the CD-ROM to print disks on cardstock or paper to cut out.) Make sure that each pair of students has a protractor, a straightedge, and a pair of scissors. Most important, give each pair of students two angle measures totaling 360 degrees.

The activity sheet directs the students to construct one of their angles as a central angle of an uncut disk. To do this, they must identify the center of the disk. Suggest ways to do this:

1. Fold the disk in half, carefully matching up edges of the disk. The fold line is a diameter of the circle. Make a second fold in the same way. The intersection of the fold lines is the center of the circle.

2. Use a straightedge to draw any chord on the circle. Construct the perpendicular bisector of the chord. Draw a second chord and construct its perpendicular bisector. The intersection of the bisectors is the center of the circle (see the illustration below).

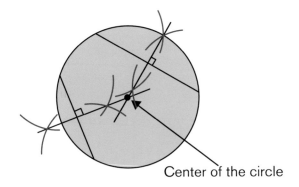

Center of the circle

The students then cut out the sector that the angle delineates, realizing that they have actually cut out sectors for both angle measures, since the measures sum to 360 degrees. They compare each sector with their intact disk to investigate the relationship between a sector and its circle. They measure each sector's circumference with a length of string, and they use centimeter grid paper to measure each sector's area.

Next, the students use the formulas $C = 2\pi r$ and $A = \pi r^2$ to calculate the circumference and area of the uncut disk. They compare their measurements for the sectors with these measurements for the full circle as they evaluate the following general claim: For any sector of a circle and the circle itself,

$$\frac{\textit{Area of sector}}{\textit{Area of circle}} = \frac{\textit{Circumference of sector}}{\textit{Circumference of circle}}.$$

The students keep their two sectors, their uncut disk, and their data to use again in part 6. However, before moving on, you may decide to spend time with the whole class, making sure that your students are prepared to analyze the ratios in the claim by using proportional reasoning. You can use a transparency of the blackline page "A Sector and Its Circle" (available on the CD-ROM) to facilitate this discussion. Direct your students' attention to the sector and circle on the transparency, and ask, "What fraction of the full circle does the sector represent?" Focus their thinking by asking, "To answer this question, should we look at the central angle of the sector? The area of the sector? The circumference of the sector?" These questions will force the students to consider a more basic question, "What does 'fraction of a circle' mean?"

Assign the following pairs of angle measures for a useful class set of cones:

30° and 330°
45° and 315°
60° and 300°
90° and 270°
120° and 240°
135° and 225°
150° and 210°
180° and 180°

Note that one pair of students should work with angles whose measures are both 180°.

A central angle has its vertex at the center of a circle.

When your students measure the area of a sector by tracing its outline on grid paper and counting squares, they can refine the measurement by using smaller and smaller units. To reinforce ideas about increasing a measurement's precision, ask your students to measure first with a coarse grid (large squares) and then use increasingly fine grids. Emphasize that measurements are always approximations. Gradually decreasing the size of the grid squares steadily reduces the error in the measurement. Templates for decimeter, centimeter, and millimeter grid paper are available on the accompanying CD-ROM.

- "Does it mean 'fraction of the total central angle of 360°'?"
- "Does it mean 'fraction of the area of the circle'?"
- "Does it mean 'fraction of the circumference of the circle'?"
- "Can it mean all of these?"

Ask the students for two of the sectors that they have cut out—the sector with a central angle of 180° and the sector with a central angle of 270°. Use these sectors to help the class think about the ratios. Point out that for the sector with a central angle of 180°,

$$\frac{180}{360} = \frac{1}{2}.$$

That is, a central angle of 180° for the sector is one-half of the total central angle of 360° for the circle. The students will literally see that this sector's area is equal to one-half of the area of the circle and the sector's circumference is equal to one-half of the circle's circumference. Thus, for this sector and its respective circle, the ratios

$$\frac{(Central\ angle)_{sector}}{(Central\ angle)_{circle}}, \quad \frac{(Area)_{sector}}{(Area)_{circle}}, \quad and \quad \frac{(Circumference)_{sector}}{(Circumference)_{circle}}$$

are all the same, or $\frac{1}{2}$.

Likewise, demonstrate that for the sector with a central angle of 270°,

$$\frac{270}{360} = \frac{3}{4}.$$

In other words, a central angle of 270° for the sector is three-fourths of the total central angle of 360° for the circle. Again, the students will see that this sector's area is equal to three-fourths of the area of the circle and the sector's circumference is equal to three-fourths of the circle's circumference.

This work should help your students understand the claim under investigation and should lead them to suspect strongly that it is true; their work in part 6 should provide additional empirical evidence for the truth of the claim.

Part 6—"Developing the Data"

Distribute copies of the blackline master "Developing the Data" and ask your students to work again with their partners. Now all the student pairs pool their results from part 5, display their data in a chart, and analyze them to see if they support the claim in part 5. The students calculate the fraction of 360 degrees (the central angle of a circle) that is represented by the central angle of each of their sectors. This work with data helps them discover not only that the ratios in the claim are equal but also that each of those ratios is equal to the ratio of central angle to central angle. With this discovery, they are set to solve the first Ritzville problem without knowing the measure of the central angle of the Ritzville sector.

Have your students extend their work in part 6 by representing the data in their chart in a graph that shows the area (or circumference) of a sector as a function of the sector's central angle. (You can print grid paper from the CD-ROM for this task; fig. 1.3 shows such a graph for sectors with radii of 12 centimeters.) The linearity of the graph will highlight the proportional relationship between the area and the angle measure. Take the opportunity to emphasize the general usefulness of graphs in revealing proportional relationships. The students' scaling of the horizontal axis will also reinforce number concepts, since the fractions that they must use—

$$\frac{1}{12}, \frac{1}{8}, \frac{1}{6}, \frac{1}{4}, \frac{1}{3}, \frac{3}{8}, \frac{5}{12}, \frac{1}{2}, \frac{7}{12}, \frac{5}{8}, \frac{2}{3}, \frac{3}{4}, \frac{5}{6}, \frac{7}{8}, \text{ and } \frac{11}{12} —$$

differ by varying amounts. The students can locate these fractions on the axis either by relating them to benchmark fractions or by finding a common denominator.

Part 7—"Coming to the Surface"

Part 7 brings the students face to face with the first Ritzville problem: how much vinyl would it take to cover the stack of wheat with a circumference of 482 feet and a slant height of 91 feet? Before distributing the activity sheet, however, you might encourage your students to explain, in writing and with diagrams, the relationships of elements of the original circle to elements of the cone. Ask them to say what measurements of a cone they could obtain directly and what measurements they could obtain indirectly, with mathematics. The Ritzville Experiments problems give them two measurements that they could presumably obtain directly—the circumference of the base of the cone, C_{base}, and the slant height, s.

These two measurements, coupled with familiar formulas and the discoveries from parts 1–6, put the students in a position to solve the first problem handily. Have your students work alone, in pairs, or in groups of three on the solution. By this point, they should be able to explain the proportional relationship between the surface area of their Ritzville cone and the total area of the circle from which the surface of the cone came. In part 5, they discovered that they could use θ, the measure of the central angle of the sector forming the cone, to find the area of the sector as a fraction of the area of the whole circle:

Fig. **1.3.**

A graph that plots the area of a sector against the fraction of a whole circle that the sector's central angle represents

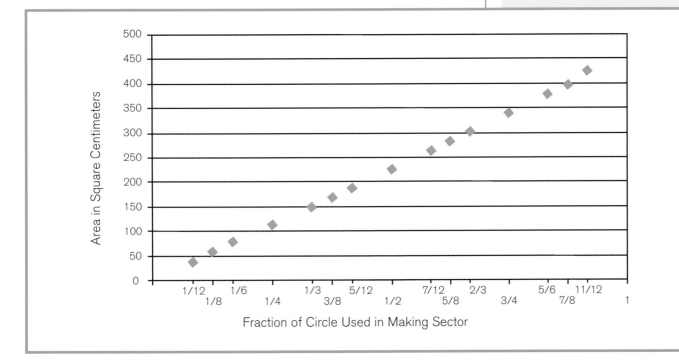

$$A_{sector} = \frac{\theta}{360} \times A_{circle};$$

$$A_{circle} = \pi r^2;$$

$$A_{sector} = \frac{\theta}{360} \pi r^2.$$

The challenge in the first Ritzville problem is working with a cone that is already formed; in such a case, θ cannot be determined directly. However, on the basis of their experiments in parts 5 and 6, the students can explain that for any such angle θ,

$$\frac{\theta}{360} = \frac{C_{sector}}{C_{circle}} = \frac{A_{sector}}{A_{circle}}.$$

Part 7 helps the students see that these proportional relationships give them everything they need to find A_{sector}, the lateral surface area of their Ritzville stack, with just the two measurements that they have, without the central angle of the sector. Because

$$\frac{\theta}{360} = \frac{C_{sector}}{C_{circle}},$$

the ratio $\frac{C_{sector}}{C_{circle}}$ also gives the fraction of the circle represented by the central angle of the sector. Thus, the students can substitute $\frac{C_{sector}}{C_{circle}}$ for $\frac{\theta}{360}$ in the equation $A_{sector} = \frac{\theta}{360} \times \pi r^2$, producing a new equation: $A_{sector} = \frac{C_{sector}}{C_{sector}} \times \pi r^2$.

This equation makes solving the problem a simple matter. The students know that C_{sector} is the circumference of the Ritzville stack, or 482 feet. They also know that s, the slant height, or 91 feet, is the radius, r, of the original circle. So the lateral surface area of the stack, or A_{sector}, is

$$\frac{C_{sector}}{C_{circle}} \times \pi s^2, \text{ or } \frac{482 \text{ ft}}{C_{circle}} \times \pi (91 \text{ ft})^2.$$

Moreover, they can use the familiar formula $C = 2\pi r$ to calculate C_{circle}, the circumference of the circle to which the sector belongs:

$$C_{circle} = 2\pi s = 2\pi(91) = 182\pi \text{ ft}.$$

They can substitute this value into their equation for the area of the sector:

$$A_{sector} \approx \frac{482 \text{ ft}}{C_{circle}} \times \pi (91 \text{ ft})^2$$

$$\approx \frac{482 \text{ ft}}{182\pi \text{ ft}} \times \pi (91 \text{ ft})^2$$

$$\approx \frac{241}{91} \times (91 \text{ ft})^2$$

$$\approx 241 \times 91 \text{ ft}^2$$

$$\approx 21,900 \text{ ft}^2.$$

"Coming to the Surface" does not directly address significance of digits or round-off error in the Ritzville calculations. These important topics may be too advanced for many middle school students. However, Nowlin (1993; available on the CD-ROM) offers a detailed discussion that can clarify these matters.

Once your students have obtained

$$A_{sector} = \frac{C_{sector}}{C_{circle}} \times \pi r^2$$

as a general formula for the lateral surface area of a cone, you may want to take them through the derivation of the general formula for the entire surface area of a cone, including the base. Some students, particularly sixth graders, may not be ready for this work. Other students, including some seventh graders, may be able to follow the steps in a very careful derivation but be unable to take the steps themselves, even with close guidance. Yet other students, particularly some eighth graders, may be ready for you to guide them through the derivation themselves. The CD-ROM includes a blackline master, "The Surface Area of a Cone," for you to use with your class as you see fit.

Because the radius, r, of the original circle is equal to the slant height, s, of the cone, students can rewrite the general formula that they have as

$$\text{Lateral surface area of a cone} = \frac{C_{base}}{2\pi s} \times \pi s^2.$$

The area of the base of the cone is simply $\pi \times (r_{base})^2$. However, since $C_{base} = 2\pi \times (r_{base})$, the students know that r_{base} is equal to $\frac{C_{base}}{2\pi}$.

Substituting gives the area of the base as $\pi \times \left(\frac{C_{base}}{2\pi}\right)^2$. The students will easily see that the surface area of a cone is merely the sum of its base area and its lateral surface area, or

$$\text{Surface area of a cone} = \pi \times \left(\frac{C_{base}}{2\pi}\right)^2 + \left(\frac{C_{base}}{2\pi s}\right) \times \pi s^2.$$

If your students have followed the development of this expression of a general formula to this point, you can extend the discussion in various ways:

- By comparing the expression with the general formula given in many sources

- By asking the students to use the expression to find the total surface areas of the cones that they made in part 6

- By applying the formula to find the *total* surface area of their Ritzville stack of wheat, supposing that the storage facility must lay vinyl under the stack as well as on it

The development of the general formula above also provides an excellent opportunity to examine equivalent but different representations of the same formula. The process can help students realize how important it is to understand what each variable represents. Many sources give the formula

$$\text{Surface area of a cone} = \pi r^2 + \pi rs,$$

where r is the radius of the base of the cone and s is the slant height of the cone. Simplifying the expression obtained above shows the equivalence of the two formulas:

A two-page template, "The Surface Area of a Cone," is available on the CD-ROM to assist you in discussing the general formula. You can make transparencies from the template and display them on an overhead projector, or you can print copies to distribute to your students for a class discussion.

$$Surface\ area\ of\ a\ cone = \pi \times \left(\frac{C_{base}}{2\pi}\right)^2 + \left(\frac{C_{base}}{2\pi s}\right) \times \pi s^2$$

$$= \frac{(C_{base})^2}{4\pi} + \frac{C_{base} \cdot s}{2}$$

$$= \frac{(C_{base})^2}{4\pi} + \frac{1}{2}(C_{base} \cdot s)$$

$$= \frac{(2\pi r)^2}{4\pi} + \frac{1}{2}(C_{base} \cdot s)$$

$$= \frac{4\pi^2 r^2}{4\pi} + \frac{1}{2}(C_{base} \cdot s)$$

$$= \pi r^2 + \frac{1}{2}(2\pi r)s$$

$$= \pi r^2 + \pi rs.$$

Some textbooks discuss the general formula

$$Surface\ area\ of\ a\ cone = \pi r^2 + \pi rs$$

as an extension of a general formula for pyramids:

$$Surface\ area\ of\ a\ pyramid = Area\ of\ the\ base + \frac{1}{2}ps,$$

where p is the perimeter of the base of the pyramid and s is the slant height of the pyramid. You might also examine this relationship with your students, or let them explore a pyramid as an assessment activity, as described on page 34.

Part 8—"Volumes Yet to Learn!"

Part 8 is the first of five parts devoted to the second Ritzville problem: how much wheat is in the stack whose slant height is 91 feet and whose base circumference is 482 feet? Part 8 serves as a pivot in Ritzville Experiments, shifting the students' focus from the surface area of a cone to its *volume*. In parts 8–12, the students suppose that they must declare the amount of wheat in their stack for an inventory at the Ritzville storage facility. Give your students copies of the blackline master "Volumes Yet to Learn!" and use it as the basis for a whole-class discussion. When the students are certain that they would need to measure the volume to find the quantity of wheat in the Ritzville stack, help them think about the meaning of *volume* by asking them what type of units they would use for their measurement. Be sure that your students realize that they now must move from working with square units to working with cubic units.

Part 9—"Can You Be More Precise?"

In part 9, the students take their first steps toward measuring the volume of the Ritzville stack of wheat by exploring once again with rice, as in part 1. They experiment with three methods of estimating the volume of a cone:

1. They find how much rice it takes to fill a cube that is two centimeters on a side, and then they find how many such cubes it takes to fill the cone.
2. They find how much rice it takes to fill a cube that is one centimeter on a side, and then they find how many such cubes it takes to fill the cone.

3. They fill the cone directly with rice, which they then pour into a graduated cylinder and measure.

This work gives the students a firsthand experience in refining a measurement by increasing its *precision*.

The students again work with two cones made from two sectors cut from the same circle, with the measures of the sectors' central angles totaling 360 degrees. If your students have kept the cones that they made in part 6, they can work with them again in pairs.

The students make two cubes (1 cm × 1 cm × 1 cm, and 2 cm × 2 cm × 2 cm) from cardstock or plain paper. They fill each with rice, which they measure by pouring into a graduated cylinder. This process shows them that one cubic centimeter of rice is equivalent to one milliliter of rice. As a result, they should understand that when they measure their rice in milliliters in a graduated cylinder, they can convert the milliliters directly into cubic centimeters.

Tell your students that cubic centimeters are usually used to measure small amounts of dry quantities, and milliliters are usually used to measure small amounts of liquid. Explain that they will be measuring rice in milliliters, but they will be converting each milliliter to a cubic centimeter to compare their measurements.

This preliminary work prepares the students to measure their cones with plastic cubes that are two centimeters on an edge, with plastic cubes that are one centimeter on an edge, and by pouring rice directly into the cones and measuring it in a graduated cylinder. When using cubes to find the volumes of their cones, the students may raise questions about how they should measure. They may wonder, for example, how they will know when to consider their cones as full, or how they should count cubes that "stick out over the top." Reach a consensus on such matters in a class discussion. Use the discussion to introduce your students to the mathematical process of creating a workable definition of *full* and carefully ensuring that their work is consistent with the definition.

The students enter their results in a chart that displays—

- the fraction of a circle represented by the sector used to make each cone;
- the number (N) of cubes, 2 centimeters on an edge, needed to fill the resulting cone;
- the amount of rice (in cm^3) in N such cubes;
- the number (M) of cubes, 1 centimeter on an edge, needed to fill the cone;
- the amount of rice (in cm^3) in M such cubes; and
- the amount rice (in cm^3) needed to fill the cone directly.

As the students examine their data, they should notice that their results for a particular cone differ, depending on the method of measurement. Moreover, they should find that their estimates of the cone's volume increase as they move from measuring with cubes that are 2 centimeters on an edge to measuring with cubes that are one centimeter on an edge, to measuring with rice poured directly into the cone. In comparing their three results for each cone, they should

Inexpensive, flexible paper plates work well for cutting out angles and making cones that are sturdy enough to hold blocks and rice.

Students can use large marshmallows and small marshmallows in place of large cubes and small cubes to estimate the volumes of their cones. In this case, you should help the students determine the volume of a large marshmallow and a small marshmallow and convert their measurements to cubic centimeters.

conclude that measuring with rice poured directly into the cone produces not only the largest but also the most precise measurement. The idea of measuring with smaller and smaller units to obtain increasingly *precise* measurements is a powerful and important one for the students to learn. The last question on the activity page asks the students to suggest ways of making an even more precise measurement of the volume of a cone. Your students might suggest measuring a "cone's worth" of sand, granulated sugar, or any other very fine substance that would fill the cone while leaving only tiny "gaps."

Part 10—"Turning Up the Volume"

Like part 6 ("Developing the Data"), part 10 gives the students an opportunity to pool their results with their classmates' results for cones representing different fractions of a circle. By exploring the variation in the volumes of cones whose slant heights are the same but whose bases have different circumferences, the students encounter important ideas of *limit* and *maximization*.

Before the students begin work on part 10, ask them to predict the size of the angle that someone would need to cut from a circle to leave a sector for a cone that would hold more rice than any other cone made from a sector of the same circle. Encourage the students to explain in writing the thinking behind their predictions.

It is not uncommon for students to predict that someone would form the cone of maximum volume by removing a sector with a central angle of 90 degrees and making a cone from the remaining sector with a central angle of 270 degrees. These students often suppose that the cone whose height (h) is equal to the radius (r) of its base will prove to be the cone of maximum volume (fig. 1.4 shows such a cone). If this conjecture were true, the students' prediction about the size of the sector to remove would not be so very wide of the mark. In fact, $h = r$ in a cone that someone forms from a sector with a central angle of 256 degrees after removing a sector with a central angle of 104 degrees.

Students who conjecture that equalizing h and r will maximize the volume of the cone may be generalizing from earlier work with rectangles and rectangular prisms. This work may have shown them that among rectangles with a given perimeter, the figure with the maximum area is a square, and among rectangular prisms with a given surface area, the figure with the maximum volume is a cube. In extending these experiences to the cones, one student said, "I think that the maximum volume will occur when the radius is equal to the height; it will be like cubing it."

However, the situation with the cones is not analogous to the earlier situations; h and r are not equal in the cone of maximum volume. As your students will discover when they compare results and make their graphs, to obtain this cone, someone must remove a sector with a central angle of approximately 60 degrees, leaving a sector with a central angle of roughly 300 degrees for the cone.

The relationship between h and r in the cone is then easy to establish. For a central angle of 60 degrees,

$$\frac{300}{360} = \frac{5}{6} = \frac{C_{cone}}{C_{circle}}.$$

But $C_{cone} = 2\pi r$, and $C_{circle} = 2\pi s$. Thus,

Students should experiment with changes in the height and radius of a cone to investigate the impact on the cone's surface area and volume. Several geometric calculators that are available on the Web allow users to enter values for the height and radius and see the resulting surface area and volume of the cone. See the following sites, for example:

• http://www.easycalculation .com/area/surfaceArea.php

• http://www.analyzemath.com/ Geometry_calculators/surface_ volume_cone.html

• http://calculatorfreeonline.com/ calculators/cone.php

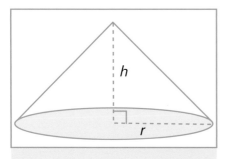

Fig. **1.4.**

A cone whose height is equal to the radius of its base

Navigating through Mathematical Connections in Grades 6–8

$$\frac{5}{6} = \frac{2\pi r}{2\pi s} = \frac{r}{s}.$$

Solving for s gives

$$s = \frac{6}{5}r.$$

The Pythagorean theorem guarantees that $r^2 + h^2 = s^2$. Substituting for s and solving give the relationship between h and r in the cone of maximum volume:

$$r^2 + h^2 = \left(\frac{6}{5}r\right)^2$$

$$r^2 + h^2 = \left(\frac{36}{25}\right)r^2$$

$$h^2 = \left(\frac{11}{25}\right)r^2$$

$$h = \left(\frac{\sqrt{11}}{5}\right)r.$$

You may decide to help your students examine this relationship after they collect data from one another to check their predictions. Guide them as they compile their results and display them in the chart on the activity sheet. If more than one pair of students has worked with the same two cones, the students should collect data from each pair for their charts. This is an excellent opportunity to them to consider—and for you to discuss—measurement error.

Each cone is identified in the chart by the sector of a whole circle that the student used to make the cone. In other words, the chart gives the fraction of a whole circle that the sector represents. The fractions appear in increasing order by size. If you prefer to have your students make a single chart as a class, you can challenge them to demonstrate their understanding of the relative sizes of the fractions by requiring them to arrange the fractions from smallest to largest on their own. In any case, the students must think about the order of the fractions when they graph their results. Here, as in part 6, they must also determine where to place each fraction in relation to the others for a consistent, accurately proportioned scale on the x-axis.

The students' graphs will show three measurements for the volume of each cone—one measurement made with cubes that are two centimeters on an edge, another made with cubes that are one centimeter on an edge, and a third made by pouring rice directly into the cone. For clarity, the students should show each set of measurements in a different color.

They must then consider whether or not to connect the "dots" for each set of measurements in the graph. This question gives you an opportunity to discuss the characteristics of *continuous* and *discrete* data. The graph plots the volume of a cone against the fraction of a given circle used to make the cone. Between any two fractions a/b and c/d on the x-axis there exists another fraction m/n that represents a cone whose volume falls between the volumes of the cones paired with a/b and c/d.

A wheat stack with a circumference of 482 feet and a slant height (s) of 91 feet is very close to the cone of maximum volume made from the corresponding full circle. The radius of the full circle is s, and the circle's circumference is $2\pi s$, or approximately 571 feet:

$$C_{circle} = 2\pi s \approx 2\pi(91)$$
$$\approx 182\pi \approx 571 \text{ ft.}$$

The circumference of the cone, or $2\pi r$ is 482 feet.

$$\frac{2\pi r}{2\pi s} \approx \frac{482}{571} \approx \frac{5}{6}.$$

The graph thus shows data that are continuous, and the students should connect the points. Figure 1.5 shows a graph produced by students in a class that made cones by removing from a circle other central angles besides those identified for the set of cones in the activity described here.

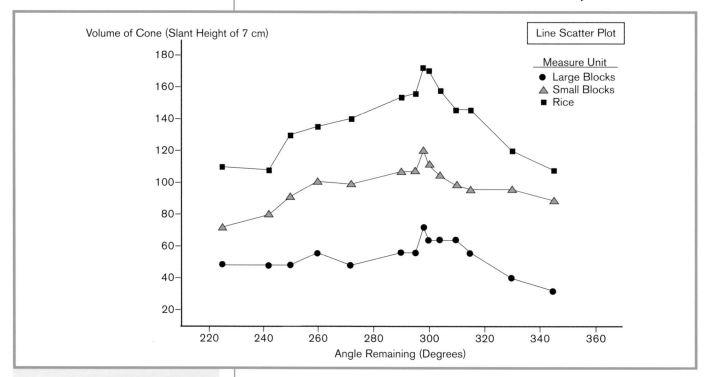

Fig. **1.5.**

A graph by students, showing volumes measured for a set of 14 cones (slant height of 7 cm and different central angles from the cones in the activity)

After displaying their data in a chart and a graph, the students should compare their predictions with the actual outcome of the experiment. Invite them to review the reasons for their predictions and consider why the cone that turned out to have the largest volume came from a sector with that particular central angle, representing that particular fraction of the circle.

The students will have removed a sector representing approximately 1/6 of the circle to make the cone of maximum volume from a sector representing roughly 5/6 of the circle. Be sure that they understand that their cone is not the tallest and the circumference of its base is not the largest, but its volume is the largest for all the cones with the same slant height made from sectors of a given circle.

Part 11—"A Second Look at Cylinders"

The experimentation and reflection that the students do in part 10 provide a natural lead-in to the formula for the volume of a cone:

$$V_{cone} = \frac{1}{3}\pi r^2 \times h,$$

where r is the radius of the base of the cone and h is its height. Part 11 turns the students' attention once again to cylinders before taking them by an experimental route to this formula.

Again invite your students to consider the context of rolls of hay stored in open fields, as they did in part 3 ("Sizing Up a Cylinder"). This context will help them bear in mind the closely related context of the Ritzville stacks of wheat. Be sure that your students understand, however, that this time their work with cylinders focuses on volume instead of surface area.

The students can work alone or in pairs in part 11, which begins by calling on them to make sense of the formula for a cylinder's volume,

$$V_{cylinder} = \pi r^2 h.$$

They are urged to compare this formula with another, which they know very well—the formula for the volume of a rectangular prism:

$$V_{rectangular\ prism} = l \times w \times h,$$

where l is the prism's length, w is its width, and h is its height. The students should see each formula as equivalent to

$$V = (Area\ of\ the\ base) \times height.$$

After the students understand the formula for the volume of a cylinder, they prepare to develop the formula for the volume of a cone experimentally. Working with the paper-plate cones that they made earlier, they determine each cone's radius, r, by using the formula $C = 2\pi r$, and its height, h, by using the Pythagorean formula (see the margin).

Next, they imagine each cone as paired with a "related" cylinder—that is, a cylinder whose height is equal to the height, h, of the cone, and whose radius is equal to the radius, r, of the cone's base. With the values that they have obtained for r and h, they use the formula $V_{cylinder} = \pi r^2 h$ to compute the related cylinder's volume.

Finally, they compare the most precise measurement that they made in part 9 ("Can You Be More Precise?") for the volume of each cone—that is, the measurement that they obtained by filling the cone with rice—with the volume that they have computed for the related cylinder. The ratio that they obtain experimentally should be close to $\frac{1}{3}$. Pooling data with their classmates should give them additional empirical evidence for believing that the volume of a cone is $\frac{1}{3}$ of the volume of the related cylinder, or $V_{cone} = \frac{1}{3} \pi r^2 \times h$.

Take a moment to discuss the resulting units in the formula. Be sure that your students understand that r^2 has square units, and h has linear units. When multiplied, these units produce cubic units. Because the fraction $\frac{1}{3}$ is simply the ratio of the volume of a cone to the volume of a cylinder with the same height and radius, it has no units.

When your students have a firm grasp on the formula, they can use it to extend their work in part 10 ("Turning Up the Volume") with the varied volumes of cones made from different sectors of a given circle. Guide the students in examining the formula to determine which change makes the volume of a cone grow faster—increasing the radius of a cone's base or increasing the cone's height. Help the students understand that because the formula squares the radius, an increase in the radius will have a greater impact on the growth of the volume of the cone than an increase of the same size in the height will.

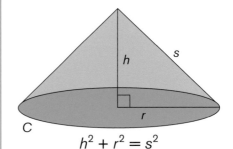

$$h^2 + r^2 = s^2$$

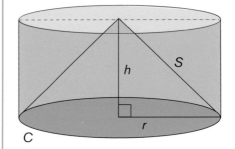

For an interactive lesson that guides students to discover the relationship between the volume of related cones and cylinders, see *Filling and Wrapping: Three-Dimensional Measurement* (Lappan et al. 1998).

The CD-ROM contains an Excel file and a Fathom file that allow users to change the radius of a circle and recalculate values easily for circles of different sizes.

With their new understanding, your students might pursue their investigation of cones made from sectors of a given circle by constructing graphs that plot—

- the radius of the base against the central angle of the sector (see fig. 1.6);
- the height against the central angle (see fig. 1.7);
- the volume against the radius of the base (see fig. 1.8); and
- the volume against the height (see fig. 1.9).

The graphs will enable the students to see which has the greater effect on a cone's volume—changing its radius or changing its height.

Fig. **1.6.**

A graph showing the relationship of the radius of the base of a cone to the central angle of the sector, for cones made from sectors of a circle with a radius of 12 cm

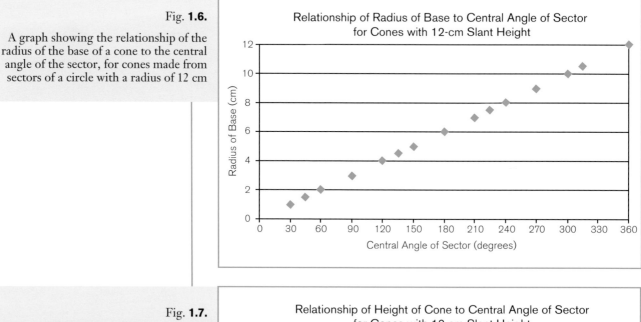

Fig. **1.7.**

A graph showing the relationship of the height of a cone to the central angle of the sector, for cones made from sectors of a circle with a radius of 12 cm

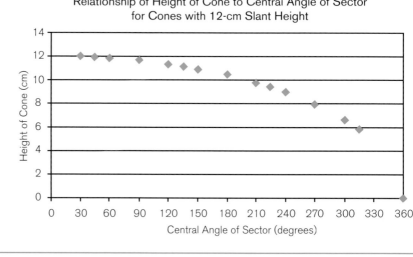

Part 12—"A Value for the Volume"

How much wheat is in the students' Ritzville stack with a slant height of 91 feet and a base circumference of 482 feet? The formula for the volume of a cone makes solving this second Ritzville problem a relatively straightforward matter. Part 12 guides the students through the process, which repeats some of the steps that they used in part 11. Students can work alone, in pairs, or in small groups on the solution.

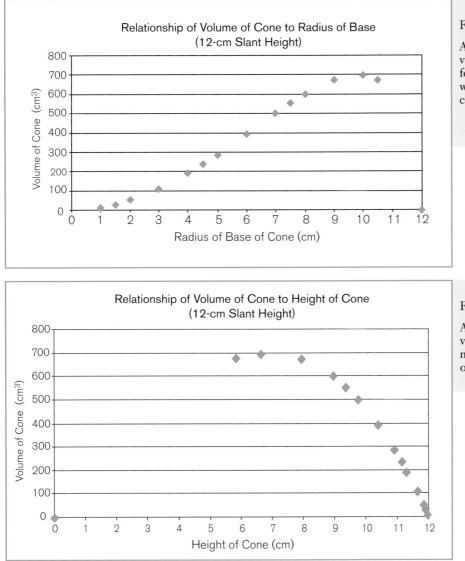

Relationship of Volume of Cone to Radius of Base
(12-cm Slant Height)

Volume of Cone (cm³) vs. Radius of Base of Cone (cm)

Fig. **1.8.**

A graph showing the relationship of the volume of a cone to the radius of its base, for cones made from sectors of a circle with a radius of 12 cm (thus producing cones with a slant height of 12 cm)

Relationship of Volume of Cone to Height of Cone
(12-cm Slant Height)

Volume of Cone (cm³) vs. Height of Cone (cm)

Fig. **1.9.**

A graph showing the relationship of the volume of a cone to its height, for cones made from sectors of a circle with a radius of 12 cm

The students know the circumference (C) of the base of the Ritzville stack of wheat. As in their work with their paper-plate cones in part 11, they use C in the formula $C = 2\pi r$ to find r, this time the radius of the base of the Ritzville stack of wheat:

$$482 \approx 2\pi r$$

$$r \approx \frac{241}{\pi}\text{ ft}$$

$$r \approx 77\text{ ft.}$$

They also know the slant height (s) of the Ritzville stack. As in part 11, they apply the Pythagorean theorem to obtain the expression $h^2 + r^2 = s^2$, which allows them to find h, now the height of the Ritzville stack:

$$h^2 + \left(77\right)^2 \approx \left(91\right)^2$$

$$h^2 \approx \left(91\right)^2 - \left(77\right)^2$$

$$h^2 \approx 8281 - 5929$$

$$h \approx \sqrt{2352}$$

$$h \approx 48\text{ ft.}$$

A supplemental essay, "Using Radian Measure to Investigate the Volume of a Cone," is available on the CD-ROM to assist you in introducing radian measure and using it with advanced students to express the volume of a cone in a formula that uses θ, the central angle of a sector forming a cone, as the only independent variable.

Part 12, "A Value for the Volume," does not address significance of digits or round-off error in the Ritzville calculations. As noted earlier, these important topics may be too advanced for many middle school students. However, Nowlin (1993; available on the CD-ROM) offers a detailed discussion that can clarify these matters.

Now the students can simply enter the values for h and r into the formula for the volume of a cone, use an approximation for π, and solve the problem:

$$\begin{aligned}
V_{cone} &= \frac{1}{3}\pi r^2 h \\
&\approx \frac{1}{3}\left(\frac{22}{7}\right)(77)^2(48) \\
&\approx \frac{22}{21}(5929)(48) \\
&\approx 298{,}000 \text{ ft}^3.
\end{aligned}$$

The students convert from cubic feet to bushels for an inventory at the storage facility. Using the equivalence 1 bu $\approx$ 1.25 ft^3 gives approximately 238,000 bushels in the stack.

Assessment

One of the goals of Ritzville Experiments is to promote students' understanding of two-dimensional nets and their relationships to three-dimensional figures, particularly figures whose edges are not all straight. To see if you have achieved this goal, you might give pairs of students a pyramid and ask them to draw its net. Working by themselves, they can describe in writing the similarities and differences between the nets of pyramids and the nets of cones. Have them explain what surface area is and how it is measured, find the surface area of their pyramid, and discuss any differences between the surface area of a pyramid and the surface area of a cone.

Another goal of Ritzville Experiments is to help students understand that the ratio of the lateral surface area of a cone to the area of the circle from which it was made is the same as the ratio of the circumference of the cone's base to the circumference of the original circle. You can give each pair of students a circle with a shaded sector from which to make a cone. You can then ask them to determine the ratio of the lateral surface area of the cone to the area of the entire circle and the ratio of the circumference of the base of the cone to the circumference of the entire circle and explain their results.

The students should recognize that the ratio of the lateral surface area of a cone to the area of the "corresponding" whole circle is $\frac{\theta}{360}$, where θ is the central angle of the sector. To find the ratio of the shaded sector, it is much easier to measure θ than it is to measure both circumferences.

The second half of Ritzville Experiments extends the exploration to volume. By the end of part 12, the students have completed a fairly comprehensive investigation of the surface area and volume of a cone and a cylinder. A performance assessment might help you evaluate your students' learning. You could ask a question such as, "What would be the optimal size of a cylindrical soda can?" The students' approaches to this open-ended question would vary, of course. For example, they might investigate the optimal volume of a can fashioned from a 16-by-16-inch piece of metal. Or they could explore the optimal size of soda cans for a display area with specific dimensions. To answer the question, the students would need to consider both surface area and volume. They might hold the volume of the can as a fixed value and explore the surface areas of different dimensions, or they might hold the surface area as a fixed value and explore the different volumes that result from changing the cylinder's height and radius. This assessment task would involve measurement and the use of appropriate units, the geometry of two-dimensional and three-dimensional figures, and the algebra of functions and their multiple representations. In a similar manner, students might explore the optimal size of a paper cone to hold fruit-flavored crushed ice for a snow cone.

Extensions

The following ideas for extending students' learning from Ritzville Experiments are just a few of the myriad possibilities. You will undoubtedly come up with many other creative and effective ideas on your own.

One way to extend and reinforce your students' skills with proportional reasoning is to allow the students to experiment with candles and their burn times. (Make sure that you follow your school's safety procedures.) Candles in the shape of cones, hexagons, pyramids, columns, and cubes are available for purchase on the Web (see the margin), and some vendors advertise burn times for their products.

In one middle school classroom, students who worked with cone-shaped candles collected and analyzed data to investigate whether all the candles had the same ratio of volume to burn time. They also measured the rate at which each candle burned in cubic millimeters per hour to determine whether all the candles burned at the same rate. Explorations of candles and their burn times offer natural opportunities to work with volumes and rates. Students can make comparisons among candles of the same shape but different sizes as well as among candles of different shapes. On the basis of an analysis of volume, burn time, and cost, they can consider what candle would be most economical to purchase.

A unit on cones and cylinders created by a classroom teacher for students in grade 6 (Cook 2003) draws on the appealing fantasy world of the immensely popular literary character Harry Potter. Teachers of sixth graders might introduce this unit to extend their students' work with cones and cylinders in Ritzville Experiments. The unit invites students to suppose that they are employees of an outfitting shop on Diagon Alley—a fictional London byway well known to readers of the Harry Potter books. The students imagine that the shop has hired them to make prototypes of wizards' hats and wands to market for the upcoming term at Hogwarts, Harry's school. A self-assessment component of the unit guides students in evaluating the quality of their contributions (as well as their partners'), their learning, and their difficulties.

Middle-grades students at a somewhat higher level can use algebraic ideas to extend their understanding of cones. They can create tables and graphs to compare the surface area with the volume for each of the cones that they have made. On one graph, they can plot surface area against volume (see fig. 1.10), and on another graph, they can plot volume against surface area (see fig. 1.11). The students can then compare and contrast the graphs. In the first graph, they will find that some values of x have more than one y-value, but in the second graph each value of x has exactly one y-value.

Wax and Wane: Purveyors of Quality Handcrafted Candles is one Web source for candles in different shapes and sizes. See http://www.waxandwane.co.uk/index.shtml for details.

 Cones and Cylinders Math Lab (Cook 2003) is a unit for grade 6 that draws on the fantasy world of Harry Potter. A condensed version is available on the Web at http://www.lessonplanspage.com/MathLAHogwartsConesAndCylinders.

This process of comparing the graphs can bring the students into informal contact with the idea of a function. For a relation to be a function, every input must yield exactly one output. The first graph, which shows surface area against volume, does not represent a function. It fails the "vertical line test" for a function, which requires that a vertical line through the graph intersect it no more than once. The second graph does represent a function by the same test.

Moreover, if interchanging the first and second coordinates of each ordered pair in a function $f(x)$ does not yield a one-to-one relation, $f(x)$ does not have an inverse. The students may observe that interchanging the coordinates of each ordered pair is equivalent to reflecting the graph of $f(x)$ in the line $y = x$. The relation shown in the first graph reverses the coordinates of each ordered pair in the second graph, but the result is not a one-to-one relation. Thus, it is not the inverse of the function shown in the second graph, which has no inverse.

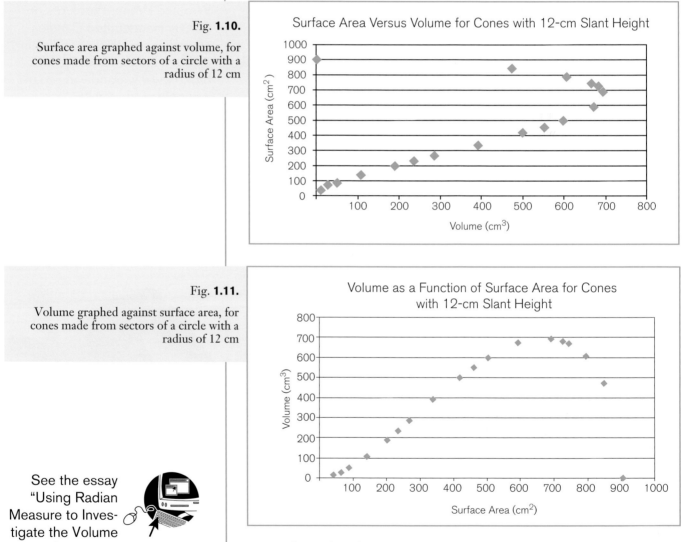

Fig. **1.10.**

Surface area graphed against volume, for cones made from sectors of a circle with a radius of 12 cm

Fig. **1.11.**

Volume graphed against surface area, for cones made from sectors of a circle with a radius of 12 cm

See the essay "Using Radian Measure to Investigate the Volume of a Cone" on the CD-ROM to extend students' thinking about the cone of maximum volume that they can form from a sector of a given circle.

As indicated in the margin of the discussion of part 11 ("A Second Look at Cylinders"), algebra students can apply ideas about radian measure to develop a formula for the volume of a cone that uses θ, the central angle of the sector from which the cone is formed, as the only independent variable. The CD-ROM includes an essay, "Using Radian

Navigating through Mathematical Connections in Grades 6–8

Measure to Investigate the Volume of a Cone," to assist you in presenting this extension. Students who are sufficiently advanced can use radian measure to extend their understanding of the cone of maximum volume that they can make from a sector of a given circle.

Students can also extend their thinking by considering the significance of digits and round-off error in their calculations of the surface area and volume of their Ritzville stack of wheat. Nowlin (1993; available on the CD-ROM) in fact devotes considerable attention to this matter in his presentation of the Ritzville pyramids. Middle school science and mathematics classes often give students their first exposure to ideas about significant digits, measurement error, and methods of taking error into account. Teachers whose students are ready for these important topics can use Nowlin's discussion to tie these ideas to the calculations in Ritzville Experiments.

For an extension that will expose algebra students to a completely different real-world setting, consider an assessment from Mathematics: Modeling Our World, Course 1 (COMAP, 1998). Here the students consider the changing base and volume of "Mount Trashmore," an ever-growing, manmade, cone-shaped mountain composed of a mixture of trucked-in trash and soil. They develop recursive equations to determine how much refuse arrives at the site each day and how many truckloads of dirt they would need to bring in and mix with the trash to maintain the correct ratio of refuse to soil in the "mountain." They explore this situation with equations, tables, and graphs, and in writing.

To give your students an opportunity to consider surface area as well as volume in this new context, you might have them investigate how much grass seed they would need to cover Mount Trashmore, assuming that a wheelbarrow holds a given number of pounds of seed, which will cover a given area in grass. The students can then develop a recursive equation to determine how many wheelbarrows of seed it would take, in theory, to cover Mount Trashmore each day until the day when Mount Trashmore is no longer used for disposal of trash and can actually be seeded to be covered in grass.

Nowlin (1993; available on the CD-ROM) details how to treat round-off error when computing the surface area and volume of a stack of wheat from direct measurements of the stack's slant height and the circumference of its base.

"Assessment 6.2: Mount Trashmore" (COMAP 1998) lets students apply the geometry of a cone in the real-world context of trash disposal.

Conclusion

Traditionally, different strands of school mathematics have been taught as different topics. Mathematics curricula have presented algebra as a separate topic from geometry, and probability and statistics have appeared as topics on their own. As a result of encountering mathematical topics in isolation from one another, students often fail to see mathematics as an interconnected body of knowledge that they can draw on to investigate and solve problems from a wide variety of areas—both within mathematics and outside it.

Ritzville Experiments, the multipart activity in chapter 1, brings in ideas and methods from diverse areas of mathematics to illuminate mathematics problems embedded in an accessible read-world context. Such activities can demonstrate the intricate network of interconnections within mathematics and their usefulness and power in problem solving.

Students who understand mathematics as a set of connected ideas are much better prepared to use mathematics to model and solve problems from science, social studies, fine arts, industrial arts, and other disciplines. Chapter 2 presents a sampling of activities that demonstrate ways of helping students make these connections between mathematics and other areas of experience.

NAVIGATING *through* MATHEMATICAL CONNECTIONS

Chapter 2

Making Connections between Mathematics and Other Disciplines

One of the goals of this book is to help teachers offer middle school students meaningful experiences with mathematics that will lead to greater understanding of and appreciation for applications of mathematics in other disciplines. In discussing the Learning Principle, *Principles and Standards for School Mathematics* (NCTM, 2000) asserts that "learning with understanding is essential to enable students to solve the new kinds of problems they will inevitably face in the future" (p. 21).

"Students must learn mathematics with understanding, actively building new knowledge from experience and prior knowledge."

(The Learning Principle, NCTM 2000, p. 20)

Learning about Applications of Mathematics in Other Areas

This chapter presents seven explorations that can help students see how mathematics connects with other disciplines. At the same time, the activities emphasize how ideas and concepts are related within mathematics. Some of the activities highlight concepts that are essential to a solid mathematical foundation, such as *area* and *volume*. Others introduce students to the use of mathematics in the real world. Brief descriptions of the activities follow:

- *How Does the Shuttle Shape Up?* explores perimeter and area, emphasizing measurement concepts that a later activity, The *Holes* Difference, also calls into play. Each of these activities can be effective on its own, but students can benefit from the opportunity to see the mathematical connections between ideas in the two.

- *Marvels of Flight* directs teachers to use an activity in the Emmy-winning series NASA CONNECT to help students collect and analyze data about the performance of different wing shapes.

- *Dinosaurs and Scaling* invites students to use a scale factor to determine real-life measurements of the small dinosaur Anchisaurus and also introduces a second scaling process that paleontologists use, called *elastic scaling*, which reflects the extra thickness of weight-bearing bones.

- The *Holes* Difference explores mathematics suggested by the plot of Louis Sachar's Newbery-winning novel *Holes*. The activity connects mathematics and literature, enriching the students' consideration of ideas in both disciplines.

- *Fingerprinting Lab* shows students some of the mathematics of the forensic science that has been essential to criminologists for more than a hundred years.

- *Who Committed the Crime?* again allows students to explore the mathematics of forensic crime solving as they inspect the shoeprints and stride length of a classroom "thief."

- *How Many Fish in the Pond?* guides students in learning about the mathematics that supports population estimates based on the capture-recapture sampling method.

Different types of activities can engage students at different levels. All the activities in chapter 2 present tasks that emphasize the importance of mathematical modeling as a problem-solving approach. You can develop the activities in various ways that will encourage your students to see the power of mathematical connections in the world around them.

Encouraging Classroom Discourse

As you help your students discover connections, make the most of opportunities for classroom discourse. Be mindful of the following advice from *Professional Standards for Teaching Mathematics* (NCTM 1991):

> The teacher of mathematics should orchestrate discourse by—
>
> - posing questions and tasks that elicit, engage, and challenge each student's thinking;
>
> - listening carefully to students' ideas;

- asking students to clarify and justify their ideas orally and in writing;

- deciding what to pursue in depth from among the ideas that students bring up during a discussion;

- deciding when and how to attach mathematical notation and language to students' ideas;

- deciding when to provide information, when to clarify an issue, when to model, when to lead, and when to let a student struggle with a difficulty;

- monitoring students' participation in discussions and deciding when and how to encourage each student to participate. (p. 35)

Consider these suggestions as you guide your students through the activities that follow.

Mathematics Teaching Today: Improving Practice, Improving Student Learning (NCTM 2007) expands the activities for orchestrating discourse by adding two items to the list:

- Encouraging and accepting the use of multiple representations;

- Making available tools for explorations and analysis (p. 45).

How Does the Shuttle Shape Up?

Goals

- Explore strategies for finding the perimeter of an irregular geometric shape
- Explore strategies for finding the area of an irregular geometric shape
- Discuss and evaluate the efficiency of various strategies

Materials and Equipment

For each student—

- A copy of each of the following blackline masters:
  - "Shuttle Silhouette"
  - "Sizing the Silhouette"
- A calculator
- A ruler (calibrated in inches and centimeters)

For the teacher—

- An overhead projector
- One or two blank transparencies
- Several transparencies of the blackline master "Shuttle Silhouette"

pp. 127; 128

Learning Environment

Students work by themselves or in groups of two or three to investigate the perimeter and area of the silhouette of the space shuttle shown in the blackline master "Shuttle Silhouette." Then the teacher engages the students in a class discussion designed to promote their understanding of the concepts of perimeter and area. The teacher asks questions to probe their prior knowledge and understanding, correct any misconceptions, and promote sense making about perimeter and area.

Prior Knowledge or Experience

- An understanding of, and some work with, perimeter and area
- An understanding of the idea that area is two-dimensional and is measured in square units
- Some experience in finding the area of a shape by partitioning it into component shapes and adding their areas together
- An understanding of the fact that the diagonal of a square is longer than a side
- An understanding of, and some work with, a line of symmetry

Classroom Activities for "Learning and Teaching Measurement" (NCTM 2003), *Measurement in the Middle Grades* (Geddes et al. 1994), and *Navigating through Geometry in Grades 6–8* (Pugalee et al. 2002) all include useful activities related to area and perimeter.

This activity is adapted from Borasi and Fonzi (2002).

Overview

The students find the perimeter and area of a silhouette of a space shuttle. They consider how these two measurements differ, recalling that area is the measurement of a region and is reported in square units, and perimeter is the distance around a region and is reported in linear units. They focus on dividing the irregular silhouette into different polygons, making important connections to geometry. If they know area formulas for particular shapes from previous work, they can apply those formulas and find relationships among them. The teacher can orchestrate a whole-class discussion to help the students make these connections.

The students also face the dilemma of determining the length of a segment on the grid that is neither horizontal nor vertical and so is not measurable by counting linear grid units. This problem can help the students recognize the usefulness of the Pythagorean theorem, a discussion of which could conclude students' consideration of the problem.

Explorations such as this one can build a conceptual understanding that can serve as a foundation for constructing or understanding formulas for area and perimeter. The activity helps students make many connections within mathematics as well as see the importance of mathematics in other fields, such as aerospace design.

Discussion

Measurement is a very important concept in mathematical modeling. Investigations in which students encounter irregular shapes prepare them for the types of measurement problems that they are likely to encounter in real-world experiences. This activity engages students in thinking processes that will support their work with mathematical models that involve area and perimeter.

Before beginning the activity, students may need to review the concepts of perimeter and area. Several sources for excellent activities about area and perimeter are identified in the margin. Some of these activities are available on the CD-ROM that accompanies this book.

Also on the CD-ROM is the article "Understanding Student Responses to Open-Ended Tasks" (Moskal 2000), which includes a discussion of the problem shown in figure 2.1. Teressa has cut paper to make a square that is eight centimeters on a side and an isosceles right triangle with legs that are eight centimeters. She creates a new, irregular six-sided shape for an art project by gluing her triangle and square together so that parts of the two overlap. The problem asks for the area of her

The activity Reasoning about the Pythagorean Theorem in Navigating through Geometry in Grades 6–8 (Pugalee et al. 2002, pp. 28–29; 95) uses an area model to familiarize students with the theorem.

 Three activities from *Classroom Activities for "Learning and Teaching Measurement"* (NCTM 2003) appear on the CD-ROM: "Measuring the Mountain State" (Hodgson 2003), "Creating Rabbit Pens" (Smith and Boston 2003), and "Perimeter and Area of Similar Figures" (Enderson 2003).

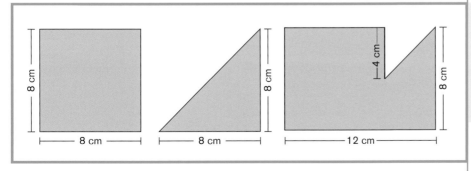

Fig. **2.1.**

A problem (from Moskal 2000) to reinforce concepts of area and introduce ways of thinking about areas of irregular shapes

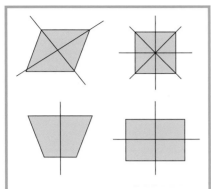

A line of symmetry cuts a figure into two parts that are congruent. The parts are *reflections*, or mirror images, of each other.

Students who need additional practice with area can work with the Areas in Geometry applets in the Interactive Geometry Dictionary at NCTM's Illuminations Web site to reinforce their understanding of the relationships among the areas of rectangles, triangles, and parallelograms. See http:// illuminations.nctm.org/ ActivityDetail.aspx?id=21.

resulting shape. You can use this problem to reinforce key mathematical concepts related to area and to introduce ways of reasoning about areas of irregular shapes.

Students should also be familiar with several important mathematical ideas before engaging in the activity. They should recognize that the diagonal of a square is longer than the side. They should also know what a line of symmetry is and have found lines of symmetry in simple cases (see the margin). The shuttle silhouette has one line of symmetry, which the students can use to help find its perimeter and area. The figure's symmetry assures the students that each component polygon on one side of the line of symmetry has a congruent counterpart on the other side.

Engage

To encourage your students to begin thinking about the concepts of perimeter and area in relation to irregular shapes, represent the following problem about two lakes on an overhead transparency:

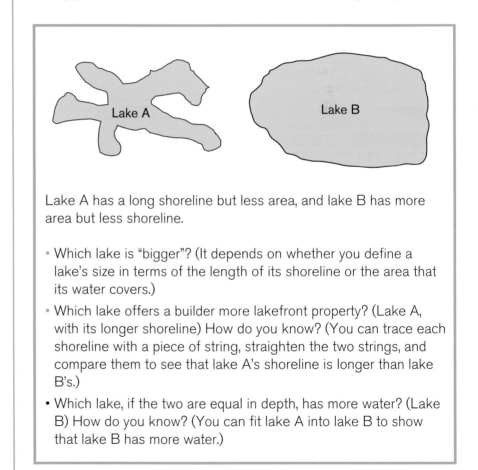

Lake A has a long shoreline but less area, and lake B has more area but less shoreline.

- Which lake is "bigger"? (It depends on whether you define a lake's size in terms of the length of its shoreline or the area that its water covers.)

- Which lake offers a builder more lakefront property? (Lake A, with its longer shoreline) How do you know? (You can trace each shoreline with a piece of string, straighten the two strings, and compare them to see that lake A's shoreline is longer than lake B's.)

- Which lake, if the two are equal in depth, has more water? (Lake B) How do you know? (You can fit lake A into lake B to show that lake B has more water.)

Facilitate a discussion of the perimeters and areas of the lakes and how the students might find measurements for each, including what kind of units they would use.

Explore

Give each student copies of the blackline masters "Shuttle Silhouette" and "Sizing the Silhouette." Note that the shape shown on "Shuttle Silhouette" does not represent the lines or proportions of an actual space shuttle faithfully or precisely. Instead, it suggests the shape of a shuttle in a geometric figure that will facilitate an interesting exploration of area and perimeter for middle school students.

You can ask your students to work alone on the activity (in class or at home) or in groups of two or three. "Sizing the Silhouette" asks the students to find the perimeter of the shape in "Shuttle Silhouette" in linear grid units and the area in square grid units. They should draw on the outline of the shuttle to show how they made their measurements and then explain their work in words. They should say whether they think their measurements are accurate and comment on their precision.

As your students work, encourage them to communicate with one another about how they are thinking about the problems. Students should be urged to "formulate explanations" and "reflect on their own understanding and on the ideas of others" (NCTM 2000, p. 272).

Explain

After your students have answered all the questions on "Sizing the Silhouette," conduct a whole-class discussion on finding the perimeter and area of the shuttle's silhouette. Students should be encouraged to explain their methods, perhaps going to an overhead projector and writing on transparency copies of "Shuttle Silhouette" to demonstrate their approaches. As your students present their work, ask them questions like the following:

- "When you were finding the perimeter of the silhouette, how did you count the length of segments in the outline that are not horizontal or vertical on the grid?"

- "Does the silhouette have a line of symmetry? Is so, where is it? How could a line of symmetry help you find the silhouette's perimeter or area? Is there more than one line of symmetry?"

A visible record of the students' methods, written on a side board or chart paper, can be useful as the students work through all the activities in this chapter. This record can include any formulas that students remember from previous work with area and perimeter. Once you have listed all the strategies that your students used, ask questions such as these:

- "What strategies seemed most efficient? Least efficient?"

- "What did you learn by hearing other people's strategies?"

Students are likely to come up with many strategies for finding the perimeter and area of the shuttle. Of course, a very simple way to find the area of the silhouette is to count the number of square units inside the outline, estimating in cases where the silhouette does not occupy full squares on the grid. Students will probably use a variety of more sophisticated strategies, as well. For example, a student may make a "ruler" by cutting a row of squares from the bottom of the grid and using it to measure segments of the outline that are neither horizontal nor vertical on the grid. To measure the perimeter or the area, students may use the line of symmetry, which will allow them to find half the measurement and then multiply by 2.

Alternatively, students might make use of the line of symmetry to find the area of half of the silhouette by decomposing it into rectangles (one with rounded corners), triangles, and a trapezoid. They can find

Areas of Irregular Polygons, an interactive applet on the accompanying CD-ROM, introduces students to finding the area of irregular polygons.

the areas of all of those shapes and add them together. Figure 2.2a shows the line of symmetry in the silhouette, and figure 2.2b shows how a student might divide half of the silhouette into component shapes. The shaded region shows an overlapping area that the students would then subtract from the area of the rectangle with rounded corners.

Fig. **2.2.**

The silhouette of the shuttle, showing (*a*) the line of symmetry, and (*b*) half the area of the silhouette decomposed into component shapes

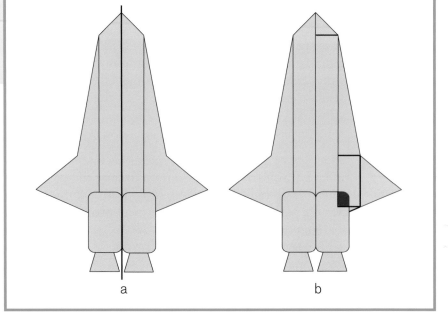

a   b

Evaluate

Observe the strategies that your students employ as they work. Do they decompose the silhouette of the shuttle into familiar shapes? Do they use a formula to find a shape's area? Interview students informally as they work, asking them to explain what area and perimeter are and how they are finding the measurements.

You can collect the students' work and assess it formally, weighing the following elements according to a rubric (see figure 2.3):

- The student's approach
- The mathematical accuracy of the student's solution
- How well the student's solution strategy is illustrated or explained

Evaluate the students as they discuss their procedures for finding both area and perimeter. Check to see that they count every side in their measurements of the perimeter. An interesting conversation might develop about whether or not to count the lines inside the shuttle outline as part of the perimeter. Discuss why those lines should not count in a calculation of the perimeter.

The perimeter is approximately 104 units, and the area is approximately 345 square units. Be sure that your students understand why the measurements are approximations. Emphasize that all measurements are approximations—even a measurement that a student obtains for a diagonal segment of the silhouette by using the Pythagorean theorem. The next activity, Marvels of Flight, provides more discussion of the difficulties of obtaining precise measurements.

	Level 1	Level 2	Level 3	Level 4
Approach	Is disorganized, with no system or logical presentation.	Shows evidence of a system, but the organization is difficult to follow.	Is systematic, providing an organized presentation, but lacks clarity.	Is highly systematic and well organized, providing a clear and concise presentation.
Mathematical accuracy	Includes many mathematical errors that contribute to incorrect conclusions.	Includes some computational errors but essentially accurate conclusions.	Includes very few computational errors, with correct conclusions or solutions.	Includes no computational errors, with solutions or conclusions clearly following from approach.
Explanation	Offers little or no explanation or an explanation that is unrelated to the problem.	Offers an explanation, but it is difficult to follow.	Offers an explanation that is generally clear, but the thinking processes are not adequately described.	Offers an explanation and a description of the thinking processes that are sound and easy to follow.

Fig. **2.3.**

A possible scoring rubric for the activity How Does the Shuttle Shape Up? (adapted from Danielson [1997])

Ferrer and others (2001; available on the CD-ROM) present a variety of activities that students can use successfully to develop a conceptual understanding of the relationship between perimeter and area.

Extend

To extend your students' understanding of the strategies that they have learned, let them create other irregular shapes and apply these methods to determine areas and perimeters. Another very natural sequel to the activity would be an exploration of the Pythagorean theorem. After their work in measuring the perimeter and area of the shuttle's silhouette, the students should be ready to appreciate the usefulness of this theorem in determining length and area in a right triangle.

Students can extend their work in another way by exploring the relationships between area and perimeter. For example, they could investigate the possible perimeters of a rectangle that has a fixed area. What are the possible dimensions of a rectangle with an area of 18 square units, for instance? Conversely, they could investigate the possible areas of a rectangle that has a fixed perimeter.

The orbiter of the space shuttle has a length of 122 feet and a wingspan of 78 feet (see http://www.nasa.gov/returntoflight/system/system_Orbiter.html). The ratio of wingspan to length (0.639) in the orbiter is thus reasonably close to the same ratio in the drawing on the activity sheet (0.667). If you wish, you can engage your students in using either length or wingspan to calculate the scale factor of the silhouette to the actual space shuttle orbiter. This extension will involve the students in measuring length or wingspan in the drawing in feet. Note that the students focus on scale factors in the activity Dinosaurs and Scaling (see pp. 54–58).

An online "e-example" supporting *Principles and Standards for School Mathematics* can help students who are familiar with the Pythagorean theorem develop a better understanding of it. See http://standards.nctm.org/document/eexamples/chap6/6.5/index.htm.

The activity "Let's Go Home" (Souhrada 2001; available on the CD-ROM) lets students use their understanding of area to solve problems about painting and carpeting some rooms of a house.

Marvels of Flight

Goal

Work with the NASA CONNECT activity "Geometry and Algebra: The Future Flight Equation" to test wing shapes and investigate the relationship between their geometry and performance in flight

Materials and Equipment

NASA CONNECT educators' guide (available in PDF format on the Web; see the margin), which provides printable data sheets and templates for planes and specifies materials, including—

- Styrofoam meat trays
- Measuring tapes
- Calculators
- Masking tape
- Stop watches (optional)

Learning Environment

The NASA CONNECT activity suggests that students work in groups of four to collect and analyze data to draw conclusions and make inferences, in the process gaining essential skills for developing mathematical models to describe real-world phenomena.

Prior Knowledge and Experience

- Experience in collecting data in meaningful everyday situations
- Experience in looking for relationships among data
- Experience in measuring with a tape measure
- Familiarity with the metric system (though students may not yet have a well-developed system of reference for comparing metric and standard units of measure)

Overview

The NASA CONNECT activity involves inquiry and collaboration as students work in teams to test different wing designs, collect data, analyze them, and draw conclusions. The students collect information on the area of each type of wing, the wingspan, the *root chord*, and the *tip chord* (see the illustration). The root chord is the width of the wing on the line of intersection with the plane's fuselage, and the tip chord is the width of the tip of the wing. For each wing, students will also calculate the *average chord width*, which is the average of the root and tip chords. The students then use this information about a wing type to compute its *aspect ratio*, or the ratio of the wingspan to the average chord.

The students conduct launches of the test planes with the various wing designs. They measure and record

A complete educators guide for the NASA CONNECT activity "Geometry and Algebra: The Future Flight Equation" is available in PDF format at http://connect.larc.nasa.gov/connect_bak/pdf/0l_2.pdf.

the distance that each plane travels in each test flight. They then use their data to select the wing with the best performance.

Justification of conclusions is an important part of this process. As a culminating activity, the students design their own experimental wing on the basis of their data on the various wing designs.

By engaging different groups in a common mission, tasks such as this one provide excellent opportunities for teachers to help students appreciate the need for collaborative work. Teachers may want to review classroom expectations for working in groups, since this activity requires students to be out of their seats simulating flights and collecting data.

Discussion

Flight has always fascinated humankind. The first flight in an airplane—Orville Wright's twelve-second flight traveling 120 feet in December 1903—had a tremendous impact on events in the century that followed. Flight involves the application of complex principles of mathematics and physics, providing a rich area for finding mathematical connections to science and technology.

The lesson "Geometry and Algebra: The Future Flight Equation" is part of the NASA CONNECT series, an Emmy-award-winning educational program focusing on connecting mathematics, science, and technology. In the lesson, the students collect data on a variety of wing types. The educator's guide from NASA includes instructions, templates for a plane's parts, and data recording sheets.

If your students have not had a great deal of experience with the metric system or with benchmarks for common metric units of length, you might have them warm up for the activity by thinking about metric units. Have them identify common objects that are about 1 centimeter and 1 meter in length to give them a frame of reference for these units of measurement. Teachers may also want to review the fact that the metric system is organized on powers of ten.

Engage

Students begin the activity by determining some basic characteristics of wings of four types: oblique, delta, straight, swept-back (see fig. 2.4). Students use NASA CONNECT templates to cut wings of each type from Styrofoam meat trays, and then they calculate the area of each one, its wingspan, root chord, and tip chord. Students may use formulas for the areas, or they may use a counting method, simply totting up the squares on the one-centimeter grid paper used in the templates for the wings. Students also find the average chord (one-half the sum of the

Martinie (2003) presents some important points to consider about cooperative groups and collaborative learning.

Fig. **2.4.**

Four wing types (from the NASA CONNECT guide, p. 10)

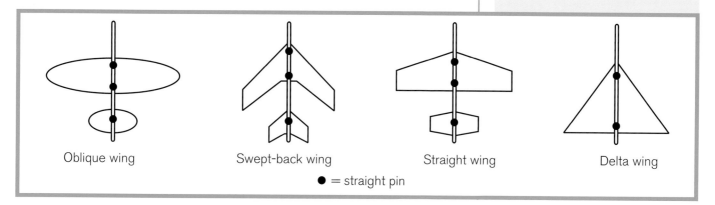

Oblique wing Swept-back wing Straight wing Delta wing

 = straight pin

root chord and the tip chord) and the aspect ratio (wingspan : average cord).

The students predict which wing they think will perform the best. They usually enjoy making such a prediction. Be sure that they explain the basis for their hypotheses. Having students predict before making the test flights engages them in relating their hypotheses to the data from the test flights. In one classroom, a student offered the following hypothesis:

> The delta wing will go the fartherest. I think that because the wing is so big it will not be able to go down because the air underneath will push up on it. It will glide easiest. The oblique wing will be mediocre. The wing's shape is so wide that it will not redirect the air like the other wings.

Students' predictions are also useful indications of the thinking that they will use later to evaluate the data and come up with their own experimental wing design.

Explore

The NASA CONNECT activity guides students in testing the four wing designs and collecting performance data. Working in teams, the students collect data on each type of wing from five trial runs and then determine the averages for that wing on speed, glide rating, and distance traveled. It may be a good idea to do some demonstration runs for the entire class.

Students may also need to discuss what *glide rating* means. A glide rating is an estimate, based on observation, of how smoothly a plane moves through the air without tilting and losing balance. The NASA materials suggest a glide scale that assigns a rating of 5 for "excellent," 4 for "very good," 3 for "good," 2 for "fair," and 1 for "poor."

This rating requires some degree of judgment on the part of the students. You might discuss how such a rating can present problems in collecting data. One process for determining a single glide rating for a flight might be to have each student in the team provide a glide rating (as well as a speed rating) and record the average of those ratings for that particular test. (NASA suggests a speed scale that assigns a rating of 5 for "extremely fast," 4 for "very fast," 3 for "fast," 2 for "slow," and 1 for "very slow.") Explain to the students that when subjective ratings are part of data collection, researchers provide training and testing to make sure that raters have a high rate of agreement in the ratings they provide. This is an example of how "reliability" is ensured in ratings.

A student in one class came up with a strategy for minimizing human error in speed ratings. He suggested using a stopwatch to time the flights. Since the data to be collected include the distance that a plane travels, he said that the speed of the plane can be determined by using the formula for distance: *Distance* = *Rate* × *Time*, or *Rate* = *Distance* ÷ *Time*. This student's suggestion shows the power of connecting ideas and concepts across different mathematical topics in the middle grades.

Students also suggested having spare wings and other parts on hand during the test flights in case one was damaged during the trial of a plane. Some students recommended not including data on a flight in which a wing broke, but instead redoing that flight. Others argued that such an accident could be an indication of the wing's instability, and therefore data should be included on *all* flights, with no retakes, regardless of outcomes. Have your class decide how to handle such a situation so that all teams approach the data collection with the same assumptions.

Fig. **2.5.**

A student carefully inspects wing designs of airplanes before beginning test flights.

After the students have seen a couple of demonstration flights and discussed data collection procedures (including a common approach for determining glide and speed ratings), they will be ready to conduct the actual test flights and record their data. Later, the activity calls on the students to reexamine their data in creating an experimental wing design of their own.

Explain

When the students have completed their test flights and recorded their data, the NASA CONNECT activity invites them to use the data to draw some conclusions about the relationship between the shape of a wing and its performance in flight. You can ask each group of students to report its data to the entire class. As they do so, you can compile the class data on a copy of one of the charts provided in the lesson guide and reproduced as an overhead transparency. The students can then examine the pooled data—as a class, in teams, or individually—and make some conclusions about the performance of the wings. In one classroom, a team summarized the data as follows:

> The swept-back wing was the best. It had the best ratings and averages overall (fives on speed and glide). It had the smallest area and the smallest wingspan, but the highest tip chord and average chord (along with the straight wing). This type of wing seems to have the design that works best.

A sample data set is included in the Solutions section (see pp. 160–61).

Students might also make graphs of the distance and speed data. It is important that students use the data in making conclusions about the performance of the wings. This work helps students understand how one variable—the wing's shape—can affect other variables, such as speed and glide. An understanding of the context of change is extremely important to the students' continuing development of algebraic thinking.

Evaluate

The ability to use data in a table to analyze differences and interpret relationships is a very important reasoning skill. Your students should carefully consider the performance data that they have gathered on the various wing types and draw conclusions based on this empirical information. It might be helpful to have students rank the wings on the basis of the entire class's compilation of data from the test flights. Working with this larger data set will help students focus on the characteristics of the wing designs that performed best.

Working with "messy" data from real data-collection experiences gives students excellent opportunities to think about data-collection procedures. The students' work with the different types of wings and discussion of their performance invite consideration of a variety of questions about how to handle situations with real data. For example, should the students establish standard procedures for the collection of the data and the conducting of trials of the wings? Should they compile data for the entire class? What are the advantages of pooling the data?

Many students who completed the activity used line graphs to depict the data from the trials. Some discussion of when to use a line, bar, or circle graph may help students understand which representation is best for what types of data. Since the data in the activity depict specific events, line graphs do not provide a reasonable format for representing the information. (An individual trial with a score of 1.5 or 3.7, for example, does not exist, and a line graph would show points between each pair of trial results.)

How students record data for distances traveled and for areas of the wings raises another important consideration. Students may have had little or no experience in thinking about significant figures. You might want to take the opportunity to collaborate with a science teacher to introduce or reinforce ideas about significant figures. Some discussion is warranted so that students understand how to record their information. They should recognize that all measurements have some degree of error. A measurement made in centimeters means that for that measurement a centimeter is the smallest reliable unit. Students might use the millimeter marks on their tape measures to measure fractional parts of a centimeter. In this case, it would make sense to have fractional parts of centimeters, such as 25.6 centimeters. Students should consider what a result of, say, 58.456 centimeters means in a computed average, given that their measurements are at best precise only to the tenths place (which would be the number of millimeters in their measurements).

A good rule of thumb is to keep computations and data to the smallest decimal place where the actual measurements can be trusted. So students' computations with averages and areas should be to the nearest centimeter or square centimeter. If students use the millimeter markings to determine distance during the trials, measurements and computations can be to the nearest tenth of a centimeter.

A good rule of thumb is to keep computations and data to the smallest decimal place where the actual measurements can be trusted.

Navigating through Mathematical Connections in Grades 6–8

Extend

The NASA CONNECT activity encourages students to use their information from the test flights to create an experimental wing of their own. The goal is for students to consider the characteristics of the wings with the best performance and try to maximize those principles. Students should conduct the same types of test flights for their experimental wing, collect data, and draw conclusions on the wing's performance in flight.

Teachers may explore other extensions with teachers in science, such as building rockets as part of students' explorations of energy (see fig. 2.6). The educator's guide from NASA suggests several other extensions as well, including experimenting with other materials besides Styrofoam in the construction of the planes and inviting an aeronautical engineer to come to the classroom to discuss aerodynamic design.

Fig. **2.6.**

Students extend their interdisciplinary study of flight by building and testing rockets as part of a science unit on energy

Dinosaurs and Scaling

Goals

- Understand how objects in scale drawings relate to objects in the real world
- Use ideas about ratios and proportionality to solve problems involving scale factors
- Reinforce ideas about similarity
- Develop flexibility in using the metric system and rational numbers

Materials and Equipment

For each student—

- A copy of the blackline master "Dinosaur Scaling"

For each pair of students—

- A ruler (calibrated in metric units)
- A calculator

Learning Environment

The students work in pairs (or groups of three) to explore the use of scale drawings to represent an Anchisaurus. Working together can be especially useful if the majority of the students do not demonstrate facility in applying scale factors in the warm-up activity described in the Discussion section below.

Prior Knowledge or Experience

- Some familiarity with the idea of proportionality
- Some experience with scale factors, possibly including an informal application of scaling in making a figure that is twice as large or half as large as the original

Overview

An investigation of the use of scale factors and scale drawings of dinosaurs highlights the concept of proportionality. The students also learn about elastic scaling, a process that takes account of the greater thickness of weight-bearing bones.

Thompson and Bush (2003) emphasize that proportional reasoning is a way of thinking that develops over a span of years. They also point out that proportional reasoning is central to the secondary mathematics curriculum and is especially important in the study of linear equations, rates, rational numbers and expressions, and similar figures and the relationships among their volumes and areas.

Investigations that involve scaling can engage students in applying appropriate techniques, tools, and formulas to determine measurements. The Measurement Standard in *Principles and Standards for School Mathematics* states that middle-grades students should "solve problems

pp. 129–30

Thompson and Bush (2003; available on the CD-ROM) discuss the importance of proportional reasoning in the middle-grades curriculum and present several activities that support the development of proportional reasoning.

involving scale factors, using ratio and proportion" (p. 240). Applying scale factors also provides opportunities to reinforce concepts of *similarity*.

Discussion

In drawing a dinosaur, paleontologists (scientists who study past geological periods through fossil remains) use what is called a *scale factor* to represent the proportions accurately and to indicate overall size. The scale factor describes the relationship between the size of the drawing on paper and what paleontologists estimate was the actual size of the dinosaur. This factor gives the relationship between the length of a drawn line segment and the actual length of the body part that it represents.

Working with a scale factor is an activity that reinforces the development of students' proportional reasoning. The concept of proportionality is woven through the middle grades curriculum and figures prominently in studies of linear functions, the relationship between the circumference and diameter of a circle, and relative frequency. This activity helps students develop flexibility in working with rational numbers as well as an understanding of proportionality.

When paleontologists determine a scale for representing a dinosaur, they also have to consider the proportions (thickness to length) of its bones. The bigger the dinosaur, the thicker the bones. Typical scaling procedures do not adequately reflect the relationship of the length of a bone to its thickness. To create a more accurate model of the skeletal structure of a dinosaur, paleontologists have developed a process called *elastic scaling* to reflect the thickness of the largest bones. Elastic scaling raises the scale factor for length to the 3/2 power to produce a new scale for estimating the real-life diameter of a weight-bearing bone. For example, if the scale factor for length is 1 : 2, then the elastic scale would be 1 : $2^{3/2}$, or 1 : $2\sqrt{2}$, or approximately 1 : 2.83. This activity gives students opportunities to apply different scale factors (see Cook and Johnson 1996).

Consider using the following warm-up activity to gauge your students' familiarity with ideas about scaling and scale factors or to provide a more formal introduction of the concept of a scale factor to students whose experiences have not included many applications of this idea. Show your students figure 2.7. (Note that the dinosaur shown here is *not* an Anchisaurus, as on the activity sheet.) Ask the students if they can find the length of the dinosaur by finding the scale factor used to represent the man's height in the drawing. Tell your students that the man in

Figures that are *similar* have the same shape, with the same angles and proportions, but they differ in size.

Jonathan Swift's great classic, *Gulliver's Travels*, provides students with interesting contexts in which to explore proportionality and scaling. Shel Silverstein's poem "One Inch Tall" (reprinted by permission in *Principles and Standards for School Mathematics* [p. 246]) offers another opportunity for students to use literature to explore rich mathematical concepts.

Fig. **2.7.**

How long was the dinosaur in real life if the real-life height of the man in the picture is 6 feet 3 inches?

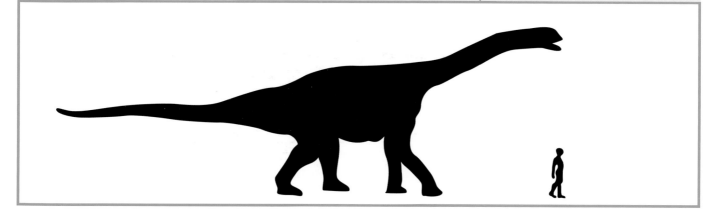

the picture is 6 feet 3 inches tall in real life. However, his image in the drawing is just ½ inch high. Have the students use the relationship ½ inch : 75 inches to find the "real" length of the dinosaur. To help your students understand the idea of scaling, ask them how many times taller the actual man would be than his image is in the drawing.

By dividing 75 by ½, students can see that the scale factor for the drawing is 150. They can use this scale factor to find the actual length of the dinosaur. In the drawing, the dinosaur is approximately 5½ inches long. The scale factor gives the multiplier to use to determine the actual length of the dinosaur: $150 \times 5½ \approx 825$ inches. So, from the head to the tip of the tail, the dinosaur is approximately 825 inches, or 68 feet 9 inches long!

Engage

To help students understand the importance of scaling in accurately depicting objects on paper, give each student a piece of grid paper, or display a grid on the board or an overhead transparency. Ask, "How could you show an animal on your paper in a way that would allow you to let people know that in real life the animal is seven feet long?" Students might offer various suggestions, such as using one square to represent one foot, and thus using seven squares in drawing the animal on paper. Others might explore a larger scale, such as two squares to represent one foot, producing a drawing that stretches over fourteen squares on the grid. Engage the students in a discussion of their solutions. It is important for them to understand that different scales are acceptable as long as they are proportional. Set up several such relationships:

$$1 \text{ foot} : 1 \text{ square} :: 7 \text{ feet} : 7 \text{ squares}$$

$$1 \text{ foot} : 2 \text{ squares} :: 7 \text{ feet} : 14 \text{ squares}$$

Explore

Anchisaurus was a comparatively small dinosaur, growing to about 8 feet, or approximately 2.5 meters, in length and weighing as much as 70 kilograms, or approximately 150 pounds. The dinosaur pictured on the blackline master "Dinosaur Scaling" is an Anchisaurus. Give a copy of the blackline master to each student, and assign a partner to each. Have the students work in pairs to measure the dimensions of the Anchisaurus and use a scale factor to find its actual dimensions.

Students should use metric units in this activity. Ask, "How many centimeters is 2.5 meters?" (Make sure that students know how to convert 2.5 meters to 250 centimeters.)

In the second part of the activity, the students explore elastic scaling. Be sure to discuss why two different scales are desirable. To apply elastic scaling, the students measure the widths of pictured support bones to determine their diameters. Make certain that they understand the meaning of *diameter*. They should also understand that their measurements are not exact, and they may need a quick review of centimeter markings on a ruler. Do they understand, for example, that 23 millimeters is 2.3 centimeters?

Some teachers have found it very helpful to discuss with students in advance the parts of the skeleton that the activity asks them to measure in the dinosaur. This way, all students can agree on definitions for the attributes that they are measuring. For example, the *length of the body* is technically the distance from the shoulder blades to the pelvic bone. The *depth of the body* is the longest part of the rib cage. The *femur* is the upper leg bone, and the *tibia* is the larger of the two lower leg bones (the smaller bone is the *fibula*). The *humerus* is the upper arm bone, and the *radius* is the larger of the two bones in the lower arm (the smaller bone is the *ulna*). Students should also discuss how to express their measurements. For example, will they write 22 mm as 2.2 cm?

Explain

The primary goal of the activity is to understand how objects in scale drawings relate to the actual dimensions of an object in the real world. After your students have worked through the activity, ask them which actual measurements surprised them. This will provide an opportunity to engage the students in a discussion about how they determined the "real" dimensions of the dinosaur.

The activity also helps students understand that scale factors have limitations. Applying the general scale factor to support bones, for instance, results in erroneous conclusions about the diameters of the bones. Students know that their leg bones are thicker than the bones in their arm. They will see that elastic scaling provides a better model for representing the greater thickness of support bones. It is important that students understand this concept. Point out that the vertebrae and tail are also support bones in dinosaurs, though to a lesser degree than other support bones. Scientists are still exploring what type of scaling best represents those structures.

Evaluate

Students are usually surprised that the actual size of Anchisaurus was so small; Anchisaurus was much smaller than the giants typically depicted in drawings and movies. Encourage your students to convert some of the measurements to customary (English) measurements so that they have a better frame of reference for the actual size of the bones of an Anchisaurus. One inch is approximately equal to 2.54 centimeters. So how high was the hip of the Anchisaurus? In centimeters, the "real" measurement is 56 cm; 56 divided by 2.54 gives approximately 22 inches.

Discuss variations in the measurements obtained by different groups of students, noting such differences as how they accounted for the curve in the body when measuring. It is likely that precision of measurement will become a focus in the discussion. In one classroom, students indicated that they used a piece of string so that their measurement would be "closer." Other students remarked on the difficulty of measuring the diameters of the bones. Students noted that these were rough estimates, affected by any errors in the reproduced drawing. Your students may also say that it was hard to work with fractional parts of centimeters, or they may point out differences in where students measured a bone. For example, some students may have measured the femur at the middle though others measured the larger part, at the base near the knee.

You may decide to develop a rule that will provide some consistency. One teacher directed students to measure the support bones at the thinnest part. Another teacher preferred not to impose even this much structure, because she wanted to be sure that her students had opportunities to discover how problems in measurement arise and may be addressed. As you evaluate your students' work, pay close attention to how they handle questions about the precision of measurements. In addition, you should listen to students' comments to see how they think about proportional relationships. This task provides a useful context for students to extend their thinking about proportional relationships.

Extend

Scaling is an important concept that students will encounter in many everyday situations. Ask your students to brainstorm to come up with a variety of applications of scaling. They might suggest maps, blueprints, models (of the solar system, for example), perspective drawings, and prices such as unit rates or "best buys" as real-world contexts for scaling.

Scaling is a powerful application of proportional reasoning. Build on the experiences that your students have had in this activity to help them extend their thinking about proportionality. One possibility might be to give your students a photograph of a sculpture such as the track and field figure pictured in figure 2.8, by Richard Hollier. Have the students work with the proportions in the art.

If you show your students Hollier's sculpture, tell them that their task is to examine the figure and use mathematics to describe the relationship between the height and the arm span of the sculpted athlete. Encourage the students to collect data either to defend or to refute the position that the depiction is accurate and lifelike. Arm span is often considered to be a good measure of height. Make sure that your students understand that arm span is measured from the tip of the middle finger on one hand to the tip of the middle finger on the other hand of someone whose arms are outstretched.

This is an excellent opportunity for students to collect data, plot them, and describe the relationships among data points. Students might make various arguments. For example, they might subtract the arm span from the height for each person represented by their data. Finding an average of these differences will provide a quantitative indicator of how close these measurements are to one another. Students might also argue that on a graph the data points for arm span and height are very close together, showing that there is little difference in the measurements. This experience can reinforce important concepts of proportionality and help students develop conjectures, reason about data, and justify conclusions.

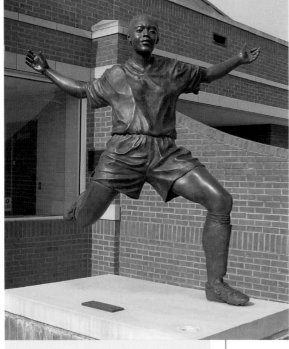

Fig. **2.8.**

Track and field athlete (sculpture by Richard Hollier, commissioned by Irwin Belk for the Irwin Belk Track and Field Center at the University of North Carolina—Charlotte)

The *Holes* Difference

Goals

- Use a situation from literature to consider mathematics, enriching both the language arts and the mathematics experiences
- Examine the reasonableness of estimates related to the volumes of cylinders
- Determine the volume of a cylinder, given its height and the radius of its base
- Select or design three-dimensional shapes that hold a specified volume
- Consider what is an appropriate amount of error in the solution to a particular problem

Materials and Equipment

For each student—

- A copy of each of the following blackline masters
  - "Digging *Holes*"
  - "Getting the *Holes* Picture"

For each pair of students—

- Several sheets of one-inch grid paper (template on the CD-ROM)
- A calculator
- A compass
- A pair of scissors

For the teacher—

- A copy of the novel *Holes* (1998) by Louis Sachar
- Several plastic cubes, one inch on a side
- Twelve 12-inch rulers, taped together to form a cubic foot

pp. 131–32; 133–34

Learning Environment

Students should be seated so that they can work in pairs, with access to such tools as calculators, one-inch cubes, inch grid paper, cylinders, rulers, and other things that might help them visualize the problem. Students work on a series of tasks, mostly with partners, with opportunities to share information with the whole group. The teacher serves as a facilitator and questioner, supporting the students as they reason mathematically.

Prior Knowledge or Experience

- Knowledge of, or access to, the formulas for—
  - the area of a circle;
  - the volume of a cylinder; and
  - the volume of a rectangular solid.

Overview

Students solve problems inspired by the plot of the young adult novel *Holes* by Louis Sachar (1998). These problems invite the students to consider a hole that is as deep and as wide, from top to bottom, as a five-foot shovel used to dig it. Then the students determine the difference between the volume of such a cylindrical hole and the volume of one that is as deep and as wide as a shovel that is *half an inch shorter than five feet*. The students estimate the difference first and then calculate it. As they work, they think about relationships among linear, square, and cubic measurements; the formula for the area of a circle; the formula for the volume of a cylinder; and "acceptable" amounts of error in measurements.

The students have an opportunity to develop an understanding of geometric concepts that are important to acquire in middle school. According to the Geometry Standard articulated in *Principles and Standards for School Mathematics* (2000, p. 232), all students in grades 6–8 should—

- precisely describe ... and understand relationships among types of two- and three-dimensional objects;
- understand relationships among the ... side lengths, perimeters, areas, and volumes of similar objects.

As the students predict results, analyze information, estimate quantities, and solve these problems, they will be applying ideas of measurement as well as geometry, along with relationships that join these two topics.

Examining the fictional context of digging holes in fact provides an excellent opportunity for students to explore measurement concepts—in particular, volume—while investigating the quantities of dirt being removed from the holes. As the Measurement Standard states (NCTM 2000, p. 240), all students in grades 6–8 should—

- understand, select, and use units of appropriate size and type to measure ... perimeter, area, ... and volume;
- use common benchmarks to select appropriate methods for estimating measurements;
- select and apply techniques and tools to accurately find length, area, [and] volume ... to appropriate levels of precision;
- develop and use formulas to determine the circumference of circles and the area of ... circles;
- develop strategies to determine the ... volume of selected ... cylinders.

The students go on to explore differences in the quantities of dirt that would be removed *over time* if two boys dug a hole each day, week in and week out, with one boy working with a five-foot shovel and the other boy working with a shovel that is half an inch shorter. The problem solving now brings algebraic ideas into play as the students analyze data to find a pattern that they can describe mathematically. As the

Algebra Standard (NCTM 2000, p. 222) recommends for all students in grades 6–8, these students will have an experience that helps them to—

- represent, analyze, and generalize … patterns with tables, graphs, words, and, when possible, symbolic rules;
- identify functions as linear or nonlinear and contrast their properties from tables, graphs, or equations;
- develop an initial conceptual understanding of different uses of variables;
- use … algebra to represent situations and to solve problems, especially those that involve linear relationships;
- model and solve contextualized problems [by] using various representations, such as graphs, tables, and equations.

In exploring measurement, geometry, and algebra in the context of considering the dirt removed in digging holes, the students make conjectures, determine the validity of those conjectures, and write mathematical arguments that support or contradict the conjectures. The activity demonstrates the potential of literature to bring life to mathematics, and the potential of mathematics to illuminate literature and enrich experiences in language arts.

Discussion

Using literature as a point of departure for the study of mathematics can give students a rich environment in which to learn mathematical concepts. In *Read Any Good Math Lately?* Whitin and Wilde (1992) suggest that literature—

- provides a meaningful context for mathematics,
- celebrates mathematics as a language,
- demonstrates that mathematics develops out of human experience,
- addresses humanistic, affective elements of mathematics,
- fosters the development of number sense,
- integrates mathematics into other curriculum areas,
- restores an aesthetic dimension to mathematical learning, and
- supports the art of problem posing. (p. 17)

Though Whitin and Wilde focus on kindergarten to grade 6, their ideas are also appropriate for middle-grades students. Carefully selected works of fiction—written specifically for readers in the middle grades—can provide engaging opportunities for students to see mathematics in other contexts.

Making connections between mathematics and literature can be a synergistic process, piquing students' interest in mathematics and literature alike. Using young adult literature to launch a mathematical exploration and give it a meaningful, rich context supports the process of mathematical modeling. Students encounter a context or situation that is very different from any that they find in textbooks, and they can apply mathematical concepts and ideas that arise or are embedded in it, bringing them to life in new ways. As students develop greater skill in thinking about how mathematics shapes the world, they will acquire habits of mind that help them see that phenomena in the world can be

Many resources are available to help teachers link mathematics with literature in the middle grades. *Mathematics Teaching in the Middle School* often features articles on this subject, which was the topic of a Focus Issue in April 2005. *The Wonderful World of Mathematics: A Critically Annotated List of Children's Books in Mathematics* (Thiessen, Matthias, and Smith 1998) includes an extensive list of references on literature and mathematical topics.

Moore and Bintz (2002) provide useful suggestions for engaging students in mathematics through literature in their article "Teaching Geometry and Measurement through Literature."

"Averages and the *Phantom Tollbooth*" is an online lesson that uses Norton Juster's popular children's novel as a context for exploring and developing the concept of average. For the complete lesson, go to http://illuminations.nctm.org/LessonDetail.aspx?ID=L204.

modeled mathematically. "Interdisciplinary experiences serve as ways to revisit mathematical ideas and help students see the usefulness of mathematics both in school and at home" (NCTM, 2000, p. 279).

The problems presented in this activity are inspired by Louis Sachar's Newbery-winning novel *Holes* (1998). The activity sheet "Digging *Holes*" explains the situation:

> Teenager Stanley Yelnats has been sentenced to eighteen months' labor at Camp Green Lake, a spartan detention center where delinquent boys dig holes each day in a dry lakebed under the scorching Texas sun. Every day, including Saturdays and Sundays, Stanley must dig a hole that is as deep and as wide as the five-foot shovel that he is issued for the task: "The shovels were five feet long, from the tip of the steel blade to the end of the wooden shaft. Stanley's hole would have to be as deep as his shovel, and he'd have to be able to lay the shovel flat across the bottom in any direction" (p. 27).

> One of the boys, X-Ray, always claims a particular shovel: "They all looked the same to Stanley, although X-Ray had his own special shovel, which no one else was allowed to use. X-Ray claimed it was shorter than the others, but if it was, it was only by a fraction of an inch" (p. 27).

The activity sheet asks the students to suppose that X-Ray's shovel is in fact a full half-inch shorter than Stanley's. How much less dirt would X-Ray then dig out of his hole than Stanley would remove from his? The second activity sheet, "Getting the *Holes* Picture," takes the situation a step further. Assuming that Stanley and X-Ray dig a hole apiece day in and day out, with no days off, how much less dirt would X-Ray remove in a week because of his slightly shorter shovel? In two weeks? And so on.

Engage

If you are a member of an interdisciplinary team that includes a language arts teacher, you may want to talk to this colleague about the possibility of having your students read Louis Sachar's *Holes* in language arts class at the same time that you and your students undertake this exploration in mathematics class. In any case, chapters 1 and 2 of *Holes* are very brief (less than three complete pages), but they effectively set the stage for the novel, describing the dry and threatening atmosphere of Camp Green Lake, where Stanley is headed only because his alternative is jail!

Read these chapters aloud to your students. Then skip to the beginning of chapter 7 (p. 26), which presents Stanley's first morning at Camp Green Lake as he prepares to go out to the lakebed to dig his first hole. Read page 26 and continue through the first complete paragraph on page 27, and then distribute copies of the activity sheet "Digging *Holes*" to each student. Assign each student a partner for work on the activity. Read aloud the explanation of the narrative situation in *Holes* (or ask a student to read it aloud, or have the students read silently), down to step 1.

The activity sheet asks the students to suppose that the shovel that X-Ray claims each day is actually a full half-inch shorter than all the others. Say, "Do you think X-Ray would remove much less dirt than

Stanley as a result of this difference? If so, how much less dirt would he dig?" Ask the students what type of measurement they are making—a one-dimensional, two-dimensional, or three-dimensional measurement?

The students may need to pause, reflect, and discuss the characteristics of and differences among such measurements. Remind them, for example, that in measuring the area of a rectangle, they are making a two-dimensional measurement. Have them identify the two dimensions—length and width— that determine the rectangle's area.

Talk to the students about circles. They may wonder what the "two dimensions" are in this case, thinking that they need to measure only the radius of the circle to apply the formula for the area of a circle. This may be a good time to take the students through the familiar activity of decomposing a circle into sectors and then recomposing them to approximate a parallelogram (see fig. 2.9). Have the students use a compass to draw a circle. Ask them to cut out the circle and fold it in half (creating two semicircles), then fold it in half again (creating four quarters of a circle), and then fold it in half a third time (creating eight congruent sectors). Then have the students unfold the circle, draw each radius that is marked by a fold, cut out all eight sectors, and piece them together to create a "parallelogram."

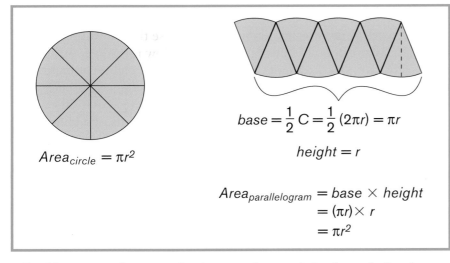

$Area_{circle} = \pi r^2$

$base = \frac{1}{2} C = \frac{1}{2} (2\pi r) = \pi r$

$height = r$

$Area_{parallelogram} = base \times height$
$= (\pi r) \times r$
$= \pi r^2$

Fig. **2.9.**

A circle decomposed into sectors that are recomposed to approximate a parallelogram

In this way, students can begin to understand the formula for the area of a circle. As a homework assignment or an extension, give each student a "piece of pizza" (a sector of a circle) from which they must determine the radius, diameter, circumference, and area of the whole pizza.

Students who have had little experience with *volume* may need experiences in visualizing cubic units. Ask them what a cubic inch and a cubic foot look like. Show them a cubic-inch block and twelve rulers taped together to form a cubic foot. (Taping the rulers to form a cube can be tricky. Make sure that the 'joints' are taped securely.) Ask, "How many cubic inches are in a cubic foot?" Be sure that your students understand that a cubic foot has $(12)^3$, or 1728, cubic inches.

Move on to the three-dimensional measurement that the problem in "Digging *Holes*" directs the students to explore. Ask the students to visualize one of the holes in the dry lakebed and identify the mathematical shape that it would make (see fig. 2.10). Once students decide that the hole would be a *cylinder*, ask them to think first about Stanley's hole and how big across it would be, and then to think about X-Ray's hole and how big across it would be. Would the two holes look more or less the same? Would X-Ray shovel very much less dirt?

Students who fully understand that volume is the space that a three-dimensional object occupies will understand what they are doing when they find the volume of a cylinder, given its dimensions. Likewise, they will see that they can determine possible dimensions of a cylinder, given its volume. Being able to use a formula in both ways is important to understanding the relationships among length, area, and volume. Through comparing two different cylinders, students can begin to develop conjectures about how a change in diameter (a measurement of length) affects the area of the cylinder's circular base and hence the cylinder's volume.

Ask questions such as the following to encourage the students' thinking about cylinders:

- "How does a change in the radius of the base of a cylinder affect the cylinder's volume?"
- "How does a change in the height of a cylinder affect its volume?"
- "How does a change in both the radius of the base and the height of a cylinder affect its volume?"

These types of questions will engage the students in meaningful discussions that can build better understandings of the relationships among different measurements and among measurement, geometry, and algebra.

Next, direct the students' attention to step 1 on the activity sheet. How many more cubic inches or cubic feet of dirt do the students think Stanley might remove than X-Ray in digging holes for a day? Since estimation is an integral part of measuring, it is appropriate that this investigation begins with an estimate. If you wish, you can record these estimates on sticky notes and save them for later, when the students get to steps 8 and 9, which ask them to consider the reasonableness of their estimates and a reasonable size for error in the estimates.

Fig. **2.10**.

A hole that is as deep and as wide as the shovel used to dig it

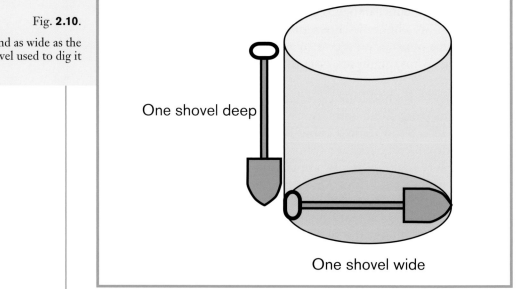

One shovel deep

One shovel wide

Navigating through Mathematical Connections in Grades 6–8

Step 2 asks the students to use a compass to draw two circles, one with a diameter of 5 inches and the other with a diameter of 4.5 inches. Check to be sure that students are setting the compasses appropriately. A student may set a compass at 5 inches (instead of 2.5 inches), thinking that the compass uses the diameter to make a circle, and not the radius. Ask students to find and compare the areas of the two circles. The larger circle has an area of $\pi(2.5)^2 \approx 19.6$ square inches, and the smaller circle has an area of $\pi(2.25)^2 \approx 15.9$ square inches, a difference of almost 4 square inches. Ask the students to explain how this difference relates to their two circles. (You might show them four one-inch squares.)

Step 3 asks the students to explain what they discovered in the process of making the two circles, and step 4 asks them to decide if they want to change the estimate that they gave in step 1 for the difference in the volume of dirt removed from the holes. Have each pair of students record their estimates (in cubic inches or cubic feet) on the board.

Ask the students, "How does an estimate in cubic inches compare with an estimate in cubic feet?" Flexibly converting measurements within a measurement system is an important yet challenging skill for students. Because one of the cylinders in this investigation (X-Ray's hole) has a height and a diameter of 4 feet 11.5 inches, students will need to consider whether they want to make their computations in inches or feet.

The fact that the students are measuring in one, two, and three dimensions presents an additional challenge. In converting a linear (one-dimensional) measurement from feet to inches, students can multiply by 12, a process that is simple enough for most. If, however, students have computed the volume of one cylinder in cubic feet and the other cylinder in cubic inches, they need to understand that they cannot compare the two by dividing the one measured in cubic inches by 12. Instead, they must divide by 1728, since a cubic foot contains $12 \times 12 \times 12$, or 1728, cubic inches.

In step 5, the students find the amount of dirt that Stanley would remove in a day if he worked with a five-foot shovel, and the amount that X-Ray would remove in a day if he dug with a shovel that was half an inch shorter. Ask the students how they can determine the volume of dirt removed from each hole. This discussion should give students an opportunity to think about whether to work with feet, square feet, and cubic feet or with inches, square inches, and cubic inches. Encourage the students to draw a picture and explain what numbers they will use to make their calculations. Once they decide whether to measure the dirt in cubic feet or cubic inches, they will have to convert the linear dimensions of both holes either to feet or to inches. Selecting a linear unit and making appropriate conversions is a challenge, especially for the dimensions of X-Ray's holes. A common mistake that students make is to subtract one-half foot from 5 feet, getting 4.5 feet, instead of subtracting one-half inch, obtaining the correct length of 4 feet 11.5 inches.

Students may struggle in converting 11.5 inches to feet (11.5 inches divided by 12 inches per foot gives approximately 0.96 feet). If students

Students can explore concepts of volume by using the interactive applet in "Building Properly Structured Mental Models for Reasoning about Volume" (Battista 2002; available on the CD-ROM).

are converting from measurements of Stanley's hole to obtain the measurements of X-Ray's hole, they might take the 60 inches for the depth of Stanley's hole and subtract 1/2 inch, or they might multiply 4 × 12 and add 11.5 inches. Students should also remember that they need to use the *radius*—not the diameter—in finding the area of the base. Stanley would remove about 98.1 cubic feet of dirt in a day: $\pi(2.5)^2 \times 5 \approx 98.1$. X-Ray would remove about 95.7 cubic feet of dirt in a day:

$$\pi\left(\frac{59.5}{2}\right)^2 \times 59.5 \approx 165356\,\text{in}^3;\ \ 165356 \div 1728 \approx 95.7\,\text{ft}^3.$$

Step 6 asks the students how much dirt X-Ray would avoid having to remove in a day by using the shorter shovel. The difference between the quantities of dirt removed in a day is roughly 2.4 cubic feet.

In step 7, students use their work up to this point to design a container (a rectangular box, or a cylinder, if you prefer) of an appropriate size to hold the additional dirt that Stanley would remove in digging his larger hole and that X-Ray would not have to remove in digging his smaller one. As an alternative, you can use empty cereal boxes and ask students how many boxes that much dirt would fill. This task allows the students to produce a visual representation that brings meaning to their numerical results. This step is important in helping them make sense of their results and compare them to their original estimates.

Your students may bring up an observation that Stanley makes in digging a hole: "The problem was that when the dirt was in the ground, it was compacted. It expanded when it was excavated. The piles were a lot bigger than his hole was deep" (p. 34). Ask your students to assume that they are recompacting the dirt in the container than they design.

Steps 8 and 9 ask the students to reconsider their estimates and what might be a reasonable or appropriate "error size" for an estimate for this particular problem. Discuss the estimates, including the range of the estimates for the class and what each one would "look like," using the cubic foot created from rulers and a cubic inch, if necessary. Ask the students, "How can you judge whether your estimate is or is not a 'good' estimate?"

Take some time to discuss the amount of error that is acceptable in an estimate. It is important for students to know that the margin of error in a reasonable estimate depends on what is being estimated. For example, in the case of a large amount, such as the number of baseballs that would fit in a hole the size of Stanley's, an estimate within 20 balls of the actual amount might seem reasonable. That is, a reasonable estimate would have a margin of error of plus or minus 20 balls. However, in a situation where the target quantity is much smaller, such as the number of gumballs that will fit in a child's hand, a reasonable estimate might be within 5 gumballs of the actual amount—a margin of error that is substantially smaller than being within 20 gumballs of the actual value.

Students often believe that the closer the estimate is to the actual amount, the better the estimate is. In fact, all estimates that are within an appropriate error size have the same value. To help your students understand this idea, you might ask them to estimate the number of jellybeans in a large jar. Reward all guesses that are within a range (for example, within 10 percent) equally. This activity will help students see that estimates need not be almost exactly right to be "winners."

Explore

Distribute the second activity sheet, "Getting the *Holes* Picture." The students use algebraic ideas in solving the problem on this sheet. Algebra becomes more accessible when it is learned through meaningful contexts. Here the students create tables and determine the cumulative amount of dirt that Stanley and X-Ray would remove in one week, two weeks, three weeks, and so on, with Stanley digging a hole each day with a five-foot shovel and X-Ray digging a hole each day with a shovel that is half an inch shorter. In step 1, the students enter data in tables. In step 2, they explain the general rule for the quantity of dirt removed by each boy. In step 3, they identify the rule for the difference in the quantities of dirt removed by the two boys.

This work helps the students see the relationship between slope and rate in a linear relationship. As discussed earlier, in digging a hole that is 5 feet deep and 5 feet wide, Stanley would remove $\pi \times (2.5)^2 \times 5$, or approximately 98.1, cubic feet of dirt each day. At the end of week 1 (after seven days), he would have removed approximately 687 cubic feet of dirt. At the end of week 2, he would have removed approximately 1374 cubic feet of dirt, and at the end of week 3, he would have removed about 2061 cubic feet of dirt. Because he removed the same amount of dirt each week, his rate of dirt removal would remain constant. This means that a graph showing the dirt removed against the number of weeks would be a line.

The rule for the cumulative quantity of dirt (y_S) that Stanley would remove in x weeks is $y_S \approx 687x$ ft^3. The rule for the cumulative quantity of dirt (y_R) that X-Ray would remove in x weeks is

$$y_R \approx (95.7 \times 7)x \approx 670x \text{ ft}^3.$$

Furthermore, the rule for the difference (d) is

$$d \approx (2.4 \times 7)x \approx 17x \text{ ft}^3.$$

See table 2.1.

"The Cylinder Problem," available online as part of Math Forum's *Encouraging Mathematical Thinking* videopaper, is another investigation that compares two cylinders whose sides are formed by rolling a sheet of paper (8 1/2 by 11 inches) in two different ways and taping the edges. See http://mathforum.org/brap/wrap/midlesson.html.

Table 2.1.
Amounts of Dirt Removed by Stanley and X-Ray in Weeks 1–5, with Weekly Differences and Ratios

Number of Weeks	Stanley's Dirt Removed (in ft^3)	X-Ray's Dirt Removed (in ft^3)	Difference in Dirt Removed (in ft^3)	Ratio of Stanley to X-Ray's Dirt Removed
1	687	670	17	1.025
2	1374	1340	34	1.025
3	2061	2010	51	1.025
4	2748	2680	68	1.025
5	3435	3350	85	1.025

The students should readily see that the rate of dirt removed in one week is related to the amount of dirt removed in one day. Help your students relate this idea to the formula for slope (m): $m = \dfrac{\Delta y}{\Delta x}$. The slope is equal to the change in y divided by the change in x. Be sure that the students understand that y is the amount of dirt removed and x is the number of weeks in which that amount was removed. Explain that in the expression $\dfrac{y_5 - y_2}{x_5 - x_2}$, the subscripts refer to the specific weeks for which the data are reported—in this case, week 5 and week 2. The students should compare this rate (or slope) to the daily rate of dirt removed. Are they the same? (No) How are they related? (The weekly rate is seven times the daily rate.) *Linearity*, or *constant rate of change*, can be identified both in a graph (which shows a straight line) and in a table (which shows that for each change in x, there is a change in y, and the new value for y is equal to the new value for x multiplied by a constant rate of change).

Also be sure to draw a connection between linear equations and proportionality. The equation for the dirt removed by each boy has the form $y = mx$. Depending on the level of your students, ask them why the equation has this form, instead of $y = mx + b$. See if they realize that in this situation, b, the y-intercept, equals 0. Prompt them by asking, "What amount of dirt was removed before each boy began digging?" In cases like this, where $y = mx$, the relationship between y and x is proportional, and the linear graph passes through the origin. In the activity, the amount of dirt removed is proportional to the number of weeks worked. For any number of weeks, students can divide the amount of dirt removed (y) by the number of weeks (x) and get the rate of dirt removed, or the slope of the line that would represent the data in a graph.

Once all your students have worked through the problems with their partners and have arrived at their solutions, place each pair with another pair to exchange solutions, explain how they found them, and decide if their solutions are virtually the same or different (this can be particularly interesting if you pair students who have used inches with those who have used feet). At this point, students might need to be reminded of how to compare cubic inches with cubic feet. Again they may want to divide or multiply by 12, when in fact there are 1728 cubic inches in a cubic foot.

Evaluate

As students work on their measurements, watch carefully to see if they are making conversions and applying the formulas correctly. Observe the drawings that they make, and be sure that they are labeling the dimensions of each cylinder. Ask the students if they think rounding will affect the result in a significant way.

When students have completed their work, ask them to consider their original estimate and the estimates by the other students. Have them assess how "good" their own estimate turned out to be and identify estimates that they believe are reasonable. Ask students to explain why they think there was a larger or a smaller difference than they had predicted.

Students might argue that an estimate that is off by even one cubic foot is off by too much, since the difference between the amount of dirt

In "Improper Application of Proportional Reasoning," Van Dooren and his colleagues (2003) describe situations in which students use proportional reasoning inappropriately to reason about problems. An examination of their misunderstandings can guide the design of learning experiences that promote students' development of proportional reasoning.

that Stanley would remove and the amount that X-Ray would remove is just 2.4 cubic feet. Others might argue that the margin of error should be larger (for example, any estimate within 5 cubic feet should be considered "good"), since the total dirt removed by each boy is close to 100 cubic feet. Both arguments have merit, and you and your students can decide on an acceptable range.

Extend

Several "what if" questions suggest themselves as natural sequels to these problems. What if the lengths of the shovels changed (you might decide to limit the lengths to six feet), but the difference between them was still 1/2 inch? Would the difference in the quantities of dirt removed be the same as before? The students must remember that the holes would be completely different. Would the ratio be the same between the dirt that Stanley would remove and the dirt that X-Ray would remove? What if the lengths of the shovels were different by 2 inches, instead of just 1/2 an inch? Would the difference be four times what it was? Any one of these questions could be posed as a homework problem or as a challenge to a pair of students who finish early.

As another extension, you might ask students to determine the amount of dirt that Stanley and X-Ray would remove in six months' time at Camp Green Lake. (In the story, Camp Green Lake closes down before Stanley has been there that long; it is unclear how long X-Ray has been at the camp before Stanley's arrival.) In this purely hypothetical situation, students can make tables and corresponding graphs of the amounts of dirt that the boys would remove over time. They can generate equations or verbal rules to give the amounts of dirt that Stanley and X-Ray would remove in six months. The tables (or graphs) would provide opportunities to discuss rate and how it relates to the slope of a line. In addition, you can ask students to compare the amounts of dirt that Stanley and X-Ray would remove over this period of time. Recording the data in a spreadsheet allows students to look for patterns in the data. Ask students to share their different strategies for figuring out their answer.

"Exploring Proportional Reasoning through Movies and Literature" (Beckmann, Thompson, and Austin 2004; available on the CD-ROM) presents interesting explorations of *Harry Potter and the Sorcerer's Stone*, *Lord of the Rings*, and *The Perfect Storm*, for example.

"Using Literature to Engage Students in Proportional Reasoning" (Martinie and Bay-Williams 2003; available on the CD-ROM) offers investigations based on *Animal Farm*, *Wilma Unlimited*, and *Jim and the Beanstalk*, as well as ideas for numerous other books.

Fingerprinting Lab

Goals

- Discover the connection between mathematics and forensic fingerprint science
- Recognize, describe, and apply patterns
- Use skills in visualization and spatial reasoning
- Collect data, formulate conjectures, and interpret data on the basis of conjectures
- Explore the use of base two as the foundation for a binary classification system

Materials and Equipment

For each student—
- A copy of each of the following blackline masters
  - "Collecting Fingerprints"
  - "Fingerprint Patterns"
  - "Fingerprinting Lab"
  - "My Binary-Coded Print"
- One or two soft-leaded pencils (no harder than number 2)
- Two unlined 4-by-6-inch note cards
- One or two sheets of regular notebook paper
- One or two sheets of centimeter grid paper (template available on the CD)

For the classroom—
- Several roles of transparent tape
- Several straightedges (6-inch or 12-inch rulers)

For the teacher—
- An overhead projector (optional)
- Transparencies made from the blackline master "Fingerprint Patterns" (optional)

Learning Environment

Students work both on their own and in a group. Working with a partner, they obtain a set of their own fingerprints and classify them, and then they work together as a class to compile data for the entire class. (The teacher may post this information on the board or an overhead transparency and encourage students to make copies of it.) As the activity progresses, the teacher takes the role of a facilitator, posing questions and guiding students as they draw conclusions on the basis of their data.

Prior Knowledge or Experience

- Work in collecting and representing data
- Work with geometric patterns

pp. 135; 136–38; 139; 140–41

- An understanding of the place-value structure of the base-ten number system

Overview

Each student makes a set of his or her fingerprints and classifies them. The students pool their data and analyze the class data set, with every student making a bar graph to show frequencies of the data. This exercise builds flexibility in working with data collection and representation.

The forensic science of fingerprinting rests on—

- geometric principles of classification;
- the gathering and representing of data; and
- the application of number concepts in a system that facilitates compact storage of descriptions of many sets of prints.

Fingerprinting science thus has many connections with mathematics (see Cook 1995).

Classifying fingerprints engages students in describing and applying patterns and involves the use of visualization and spatial reasoning. As the Geometry Standard states, an important goal of instruction, pre-K–grade 12, is to "enable all students to … use visualization, spatial reasoning, and geometric modeling to solve problems" (NCTM 2000, p. 232). The students should have little difficulty in using their spatial visualization skills to identify patterns in fingerprints.

The students' knowledge of the place-value structure of the base-ten number system will give meaning and context to the introductory exploration of the base-two number system in the activity. A binary, or base-two, system is the foundation of a basic fingerprint classification system. Each student determines the binary classification of his or her set of prints, developing facility with numbers and different ways of representing numbers. The binary classification system may pose some problems for students who do not fully grasp the concept of place-value.

Students enter the middle grades with varied experiences in collecting and representing data, formulating conjectures, and drawing conclusions on the basis of the data. In gathering information about their own fingerprint patterns and those of their classmates, they will encounter and apply important concepts of data collection and analysis. As *Principles and Standards* recommends, all students in grades 6–8 should—

- use observations … to make conjectures about the populations from which … samples were taken;
- use conjectures to formulate new questions (NCTM 2000, p. 248).

Discussion

Fingerprinting is the science of identifying visible patterns of ridges and valleys on the fingertips for use in personal identification. Fingerprints have been the primary means of identification for criminologists for more than one hundred years. Fingerprinting builds on the fact that no two fingerprints are alike—not even for identical twins. Moreover, fingerprints are permanent identifiers; they do not change with age or job-related activities.

All students should "use visualization, spatial reasoning, and geometric modeling to solve problems" (NCTM 2000, p. 232).

For more details about fingerprints and the mathematics of fingerprinting, see Cook (1995).

Engage

Arrange your students in pairs. Working with a partner will make the process of collecting fingerprints a little easier. Give a copy of the blackline master "Collecting Fingerprints" to each student, along with two unlined 4-by-6-inch cards. Each student should also have one or two sheets of regular notebook paper and one or two soft-leaded pencils. Collecting fingerprints can be a little messy. Although commercial kits are available for the task, the process described on the activity sheet, using tape and lead from pencils, can work reasonably well. Avoid using inkpads because of the damage that ink stains can do to clothing and equipment. Observe your students closely, and give them clear instructions for lifting their fingerprints. With careful supervision, they can gather the information necessary to complete the activity.

Once your students have collected their fingerprints, they will need some familiarity with the basic fingerprint patterns used to classify them. A class discussion might be the best way to acquaint the students with the patterns. Distribute copies of the blackline master "Fingerprint Patterns." Alternatively, you might introduce the patterns on transparencies on the overhead projector, possibly covering the labels at first.

Fingerprints have ridges (raised lines) and valleys that form three basic patterns: *loops*, *whorls*, and *arches*. The descriptions that follow also appear on the activity sheet "Fingerprint Patterns."

Loops (shown in fig. 2.11) are formed by ridges that enter on one side of a fingerprint, curve back, and leave on the same side. These ridges form a loop that bends toward the thumb or the little finger. A loop is identified as a *left loop* or a *right loop* and has two other distinguishing features: its *typelines* and its *delta*. The typelines are ridges that enter on the opposite side of the print from the ridges described above, which come in, curve back, and leave on one side to form the loop. In contrast, the typelines start as side-by-side ridges that go close in to the loop before diverging to surround it (or to appear to surround it). The typelines and the point at which they diverge appear in the circled area in each of the loop patterns pictured in figure 2.11. This point of divergence is known as a delta because it occurs where ridges on three sides make a configuration that resembles a triangle or the Greek letter Δ.

<table>
<tr><td>Fig. **2.11.**

Loops</td><td>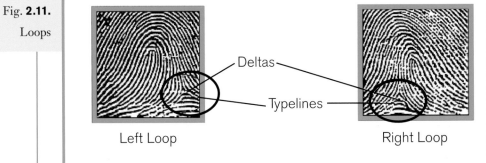
Left Loop   Right Loop</td></tr>
</table>

A *whorl* (shown in fig. 2.12) is a complete circle in a fingerprint. Whorls are formed by ridges that enter on a side of the fingerprint, spiral inward, and end in the center. A print with a whorl typically has two deltas. These triangular configurations appear on opposite sides of the print in figure 2.12.

Whorls are differentiated into three broad classes: *plain whorls*, *central pocket whorls*, and *double loop whorls* (see fig. 2.13). To distinguish a plain whorl and a central pocket whorl, a fingerprint examiner makes a line connecting the deltas in the print (see the line segments drawn in the prints in fig. 2.13):

- A whorl is a *plain whorl* if the line crosses at least one complete circle in the whorl.
- A whorl is a *central pocket whorl* if the line does not cross any part of a full circle in the whorl.

A whorl of the third type, a *double loop whorl*, is distinguished by the presence of two separate and distinct loop formations, with two *cores*. Informally, a core is the center of a pattern area; more formally, it is the point at which the innermost ridge curves back in forming the pattern in the print. Note that in the three prints shown in figure 2.13, the plain and central pocket whorls have one core apiece, but the double loop whorl has two cores.

Fig. **2.12**.

A whorl

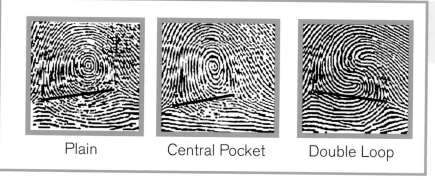

| Plain | Central Pocket | Double Loop |

Fig. **2.13**.

Three types of whorls

Note also that a line segment that connects the deltas in a double loop whorl cuts through the pattern area, as it does for a plain whorl. However, a double loop whorl is unlikely to be mistaken for a plain whorl. The clearly visible S-curve readily distinguishes the pattern as a double loop whorl.

Arches have ridges that enter on one side of the fingerprint, rise, and then slope back down, exiting on the opposite side of the print (see fig. 2.14a). A plain arch rises and falls fairly smoothly through the pattern area, but a *tented arch* rises up and falls down much more steeply, supported by a ridge that acts as a spine or axis for the pattern (see fig. 2.14b).

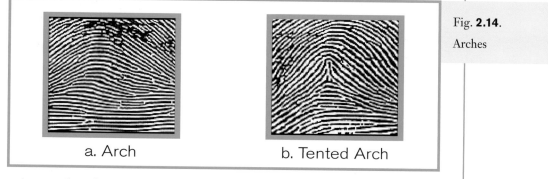

a. Arch   b. Tented Arch

Fig. **2.14**.

Arches

A tented arch may appear to have a delta; however, the formal, complete definition of delta disqualifies the three-sided configuration in an arch from any status as a delta. By definition, a delta must be positioned so that at least one ridge passes between it and the core of a pattern area. In a tented arch, the "pseudo-delta" is itself at the core of the pattern area, serving to prop it up.

After you and your students have discussed and examined the three basic fingerprint patterns, ask them to inspect their own sets of prints and think about which fingerprints they could group together and classify according to these basic patterns. Encourage them to justify their groupings by describing similarities in the patterns that they are seeing. Have the students work by themselves to classify their prints and record their conclusions on the activity sheet "Fingerprint Patterns."

Explore

Give a copy of the blackline master "Fingerprinting Lab" and one or two sheets of centimeter grid paper to each student. Step 1 asks the students to pool the data on their own fingerprints with their classmates'. Step 2 asks them to create a bar graph showing the prevalence of the three patterns in the class on the basis of the data from all the students on each of their fingers.

Students may wonder if one person's fingerprints are likely to vary in pattern. They may be surprised to learn that all ten fingers are unlikely to have the same pattern. A police officer who routinely takes fingerprints knows that each fingerprint that he or she takes from an individual has the potential to have a different pattern from the previous one. A student may have whorls on a thumb and index finger but arches or loops on the other fingers.

Thus, a frequency graph of patterns for all ten fingers for all the students in a class can yield results that are interesting to compare with frequencies in the population at large. The loop pattern is dominant in approximately 65 percent of individuals; the whorl pattern, in approximately 30 percent; and the arch pattern, in approximately 5 percent. Students can use this information to make comparisons with the class data.

As your students prepare to make their graphs, take the opportunity to discuss the difference between a bar graph and a circle graph. Point out that later (in step 5) they will convert their frequencies to percentages. Ask, "What type of graph would be good for depicting the percentages?" Students should realize that a bar graph is a good way to represent frequencies, but a circle graph is more suitable for showing percentages.

This part of the activity closes with a discussion of patterns in the data and whether the students think these patterns would be a good indication of frequencies in the general population. The students should conclude that the data from their own classroom group are insufficient to indicate fingerprint profiles for the population at large.

Explain

Give each student a copy of the blackline master "My Binary-Coded Print." In this final part of the activity, the students come up with the binary profile of their fingerprint set.

Early fingerprinting systems used a classification method that reduced a set of prints to a compact binary code, allowing the storing

The loop pattern is dominant in approximately 65 percent of individuals; the whorl pattern, in approximately 30 percent; and the arch pattern, in approximately 5 percent.

Navigating through Mathematical Connections in Grades 6–8

of descriptions of millions of fingerprints on thousands of note cards. Computer technology has greatly simplified this storage task today.

The primary fingerprint classification system uses the whorls in a set of prints to produce a binary number in stacked form to describe the full set of prints. The system evaluates whorls because they are less prevalent than loops but more prevalent than arches. Thus, they can serve as the basis for a system that is meaningful and informative.

This system pairs fingerprints in each set of ten prints, starting with the fingers of the right hand and working from the thumb to the little finger, and then moving to fingers of the left hand and working in the same manner, from thumb to little finger. The pairs are ordered as follows:

1. Right thumb and right index finger
2. Right middle and right ring fingers
3. Right little finger and left thumb
4. Left index and left middle fingers
5. Left ring and left little fingers

The classification system then stacks each pair, with the first finger in the pair appearing on the bottom:

$$\frac{\text{Right Index}}{\text{Right Thumb}} \quad \frac{\text{Right Ring}}{\text{Right Middle}} \quad \frac{\text{Left Thumb}}{\text{Right Little}} \quad \frac{\text{Left Middle}}{\text{Left Index}} \quad \frac{\text{Left Little}}{\text{Left Ring}}$$

Arranged in this way, each pair looks like a fraction, or a ratio, but it does not function conventionally in that way.

In working with a set of fingerprints, an analyst gives a numerical value to each fingerprint that has a whorl. The number depends on the pair in which the whorl appears. If the whorl is on a finger in the first pair (right thumb and right index), the analyst assigns it a value of 16. If both fingers in the pair have whorls, each receives this value. In the second pair, any print with a whorl receives a value of 8. In the third pair, a print with a whorl is assigned a 4. In the fourth pair, a print with a whorl receives a 2. In the fifth pair, a print with a whorl receives a 1.

For example, if a set of prints has whorls on the right thumb, the right index finger, the left middle finger, and the left little finger, the pairs have the following numerical values:

$$\frac{16}{16} \quad \frac{0}{0} \quad \frac{0}{0} \quad \frac{2}{0} \quad \frac{1}{0}.$$

To use the binary classification system, the analyst then substitutes base-two numbers for the base-ten numbers in these expressions, as follows: $16 = 10000_2$, $8 = 1000_2$, $4 = 100_2$, $2 = 10_2$, $1 = 1_2$:

$$\frac{10000_2}{10000_2} \quad \frac{0}{0} \quad \frac{0}{0} \quad \frac{10_2}{0} \quad \frac{1}{0}.$$

The system then calls for the analyst to add the top values in the stacked pairs together, and to add the bottom values together, as well:

$$\frac{10000_2 + 0 + 0 + 10_2 + 1}{10000_2 + 0 + 0 + 0 + 0} = \frac{10011_2}{10000_2}.$$

Students may not be acquainted with any number system other than base ten. A quick review of the base-ten system, emphasizing place value, might be a good starting point for such students.

Base-ten number	Base-two number
1	1
2	10
3	11
4	100
5	101
6	110
7	111
8	1000
9	1001
10	1010
11	1011
12	1100
13	1101
14	1110
15	1111
16	10000

The expression $\dfrac{10011_2}{10000_2}$ is the binary code that the analyst would store for the set of prints in the example.

Present such an example to your students, and examine the resulting code with them. Be sure that they understand why the classification system—

- creates the ordered pairs;
- stacks them as it does; and
- assigns base-two values for 16, 8, 4, and 2 to whorls in the first, second, third, and fourth pairs, respectively.

Do your students see that they can handily "read" the binary result to learn exactly how many whorls are present, and where they occur, in a complete set of fingerprints? Do the students see that in a binary code for a set of prints a 1 always indicates the presence of a whorl and a 0 always indicates the absence of one? Do they grasp the usefulness of selecting the base-two expressions for 16, 8, 4, 2 (and 1) in the system? If necessary, point out that—

- the base-two expression for 16, or 10000, is a 1 followed by four 0s and thus serves as a very efficient representation of a whorl in the first pair out of five pairs, without indicating any whorls elsewhere;
- the base-two expression for 8, or 1000, is a 1 followed by three 0s and thus serves as a very efficient representation of a whorl in the second pair without indicating any whorls elsewhere;
- the base-two expression for 4, or 100, is a 1 followed by two 0s and thus serves as a very efficient representation of a whorl in the third pair without indicating any whorls elsewhere;
- the base-two expression for 2, or 10, is a 1 followed by one 0 and thus serves as a very efficient representation of a whorl in the fourth pair without indicating any whorls elsewhere; and
- the base-two expression for 1 is the numeral 1. A 1 in the ones place serves as an efficient representation of a whorl in the fifth pair without indicating any whorls elsewhere.

Because the positions of the fingers are fixed in the stacked pairs, and the order of the pairs is also fixed, the binary code gives a very compact snapshot of the whorls in a set of fingerprints.

Evaluate

The students' glimpse of a binary number system in this activity can provide a valuable point of departure for a discussion of the benefits of a base-ten number system as well as applications of other systems of numeration. Such a discussion can broaden and extend students' experiences with numbers from elementary school as students think—perhaps for the first time—about other ways of counting.

Flexibility with number systems helps students understand the structure of the base-ten system. As they work with various counting systems, they gain a clearer, richer, and more sophisticated concept of place value, its uses, and its purpose. These ideas are important in helping students understand the structures of numbers and their relationships with one another. Experiences with number systems will build students' flexibility in composing and decomposing numbers.

To offer students experiences with number systems and counting methods, see "Other Ways to Count" (Fogel 2003; available on the CD-ROM), which explores the base-ten number system, the Aztec counting system (based on 20), and the binary number system.

Luis Ortiz-Franco (2001) presents two lessons for students on the vigesimal Aztec number system and its links to algebra.

Navigating through Mathematical Connections in Grades 6–8

Extend

This activity provides students with a very basic framework for understanding how fingerprinting works. As an extension to learning about the three basic fingerprint patterns—loops, whorls, and arches—students can explore how criminologists match prints by looking more closely at the points of identity (or *minutiae*) identified by Sir Francis Galton in the late 1800s.

This process involves comparing the positions of these points in two prints. Experts base the comparisons on three basic characteristics: the ridge ending, the bifurcation (or forking), and the dot (see fig. 2.15).

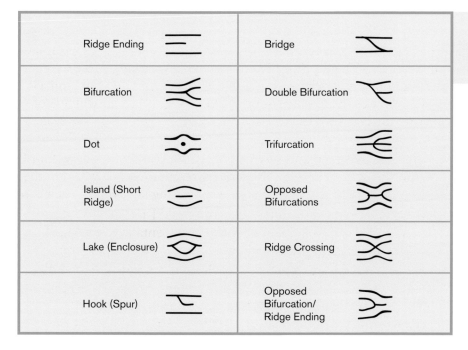

Fig. **2.15.**

Basic and composite Galton characteristics

To give your students additional information about classifying fingerprints, copy and distribute the blackline master "Basic and Composite Galton Characteristics," which appears on the CD-ROM.

The ridge ending has a variation: the *island*, or *short ridge*. In this case, the ridge ending is abrupt, and the short ridge appears as an island between two longer ridges. The dot also has an alternative pattern: the *lake*, or *enclosure*. These five patterns (ridge ending, bifurcation, dot, island, lake) may be found in various combinations and are referred to as basic Galton characteristics. The CD contains a blackline master showing basic and composite Galton characteristics.

Forensics experts may locate these characteristics in a print and search for them in another print, comparing to see whether they are of the same type, whether they "flow" or open in the same or different directions, and whether they have the same orientation or relationship to other characteristics.

These characteristics provide a basis for making a match between prints. Students will appreciate how complex the process is and the usefulness of computers in comparing and matching prints efficiently and effectively.

Students can try to locate these characteristics in their own prints. They might work in in pairs to see how these characteristics differ in two sets of prints. Students might compare, for example, the characteristics in their right thumbprints.

One teacher reports that she customarily assigns her students to groups of four or five for additional work in recognizing patterns in

Sir Francis Galton concluded from his research that the probability of two persons having the same detail in ridge characteristics was 1: (6.4 × 10⁹). For comparison, the estimated population of the world in the first month of 2008 was 6,642,931,460, or approximately 6.6 × 10⁹, according to U.S. Census projections.

Explorations of fingerprinting can help students build their skills in spatial visualization and pattern recognition. Students engage in even more complex visualization tasks when they identify and describe characteristics that are embedded in the print.

fingerprints. She makes a copy of one fingerprint, privately and in advance, from the sets of fingerprints that each group compiled earlier in the activity. She then gives each group a fingerprint that belongs to a member of the group. The group members must work together with their sets of prints to match the mystery print, determining whose it is, and which finger it represents.

Who Committed the Crime?

Goals

- Make measurements to collect data
- Create data tables and scatterplots
- Explore the idea of a "line of best fit" and use such a line to interpret data
- Understand that the line of best fit provides a model that permits predictions
- Make predictions to solve a "crime"

Materials and Equipment

For each student—

- A copy of the blackline master "Who Committed the Crime?"

pp. 142–44

For each group of four students—

- Two sheets of centimeter grid paper (template on the CD-ROM)
- Access to a graphing calculator (optional)
- Access to the applet Changing Slope and *y*-Intercept (optional)

For the classroom—

- Several tape measures or yardsticks (taped to the walls)
- Several tape measures or yardsticks (taped to the floor)
- Several transparent plastic rulers
- Several lengths of uncooked spaghetti

For the teacher—

- A small bag of flour
- Crime scene tape (or wide yellow ribbon)
- A "stolen" item (book, hat, paperweight, mug, box of candy, package of popcorn, etc.)
- Flip-chart paper (or overhead transparencies and projector)

Learning Environment

In different parts of the investigation, the students work in small groups, as a class, and on their own. Working as a class, they inspect a "crime scene." In groups of four, they gather data on one another. Each student enters the data for the group into two T-charts. The groups pool their data to create two class T-charts, which each group then uses to make two scatterplots. The students work in groups to find lines of best fit and use the equations to make predictions and attempt to solve a "crime."

"Students in grades 3–5 develop the idea that a mathematical model has both descriptive and predictive power."
(NCTM 2000, p. 162)

Ask your students what a mathematical model is. Do they understand how a problem solver can use a model to describe a phenomenon and predict outcomes associated with it? Their responses can give an indication of their experience with mathematical models.

Prior Knowledge or Experience

- Experience in designing an investigation to answer a question
- Ability to make accurate measurements in inches (or centimeters)
- Ability to make measurements that are precise to the nearest quarter inch or half centimeter
- Experience in converting fractional parts of inches to decimal parts
- Experience in making and using tables to represent patterns
- Experience in entering data points on a Cartesian graph
- Experience in justifying conclusions on the basis of data
- Experience in creating and interpreting a mathematical model

Overview

The students examine a classroom "crime scene"—the scene of a supposed theft—which the teacher has set up in advance with help from a carefully selected "thief." The students analyze the evidence at the scene (shoeprints in flour on the floor) to profile and possibly identify the thief. They obtain measurements of the thief's shoe and stride lengths as well as their own. They speculate about possible relationships between these measurements and another measurement that they cannot make directly—*height*. They collect data on their own heights and make scatterplots to examine the relationship between shoe length and height, and stride length and height. They use lines of best fit to help predict the thief's height and solve the crime.

The investigation helps the students make connections among algebra, measurement, and data analysis. It incorporates a number of expectations that *Principles and Standards for School Mathematics* (NCTM 2000) identifies in these areas for grades 6–8. As the Algebra Standard (p. 222) recommends, the students—

- use symbolic algebra to represent situations and to solve problems, especially those that involve linear relationships;
- model and solve contextualized problems using various representations, such as graphs, tables, and equations;
- use graphs to analyze the nature of changes in quantities in linear relationships.

As the Measurement Standard (p. 240) suggests, the students' work helps them to—

- understand, select, and use units of appropriate size and type to measure;
- select and apply techniques and tools to accurately find length.

As the Data Analysis and Probability Standard (p. 248) expects, the students—

- formulate questions, design studies, and collect data about … different characteristics within one population;

- make conjectures about possible relationships between two characteristics of a sample on the basis of scatterplots of the data and approximate lines of fit.

Furthermore, the investigation helps students meet the expectations of the Connections Standard (p. 402) as they—

- recognize and use connections among mathematical ideas;

- understand how mathematical ideas interconnect and build on one another to produce a coherent whole;

- recognize and apply mathematics in contexts outside of mathematics.

Discussion

Giving students a mystery to unravel is a highly effective way to engage them in mathematical problem solving. Forensics is an increasingly popular topic in televised crime programs. These shows frequently allow viewers to participate vicariously in the gathering and interpreting of evidence to identify a criminal and solve a crime.

Forensics experts often depend on mathematics to help them solve problems. An awareness of this fact can help students see the usefulness of mathematics outside the classroom. The formulation of hypotheses and the construction of conclusions frequently depend on creating a mathematical model that links conjectures about an event with the available data.

To simulate a "crime scene" in your classroom, enlist the help of a fellow teacher, school administrator, or student. Arrange to work together with your "partner in crime" after or before school to set up the scene of a supposed theft. Explain to your assistant that he or she will act as the "thief" and must take at least two steps, using a normal walking stride, in flour that you have scattered in an area of the classroom floor. After the thief has made suitable shoeprints (prints that are distinct and measurable), cordon off the area with crime tape (or plain yellow ribbon). Give the thief whatever item you have decided to claim as stolen, and instruct him or her to conceal it in a backpack, desk, jacket pocket, or whatever location the two of you decide is appropriate.

The investigation that the students undertake builds on some of the same processes that forensics experts use in formulating reasonable conclusions from evidence at a crime scene. The students use mathematics to learn more about the person who committed the crime. They engage in measuring, collecting data, creating data tables and scatterplots, analyzing data, and making predictions. Working from measurements of the length of the thief's shoe and his or her stride, they conjecture that these measurements may predict another measurement—height—which could help them identify the criminal. They gather data on their own shoe lengths, stride lengths, and heights to test whether a relationship exists between shoe length and height, or between stride length and height. If they conclude that one or both of these relationships hold, they can make predictions about the height of the criminal.

Accuracy in measurement is important in the investigation, since error can compound during analysis. For example, if students do not determine a common, exact starting point for measuring stride length or are not always careful to start measuring at that point, their measure-

Students frequently have difficulty with concepts of standard measurement. One possible reason for their poor performance on measurement tasks is their lack of experience with standard measurement instruments (Nitabach and Lehrer 1996).

NAEP (National Assessment of Educational Progress) data suggest that middle school students may understand the attribute length and may be skilled at selecting appropriate units for measuring it but do not always understand the role of the unit in measuring (Strutchens, Martin, and Kenney 2003).

ments can lead to predictions of heights that are significantly "over" or "under" the actual height of the thief. A student who measures the length of an extended stride instead of a normal stride may obtain a ratio of height to stride length that is smaller than it would be with a more accurate measurement. The students in the class should determine a method for measuring stride length, shoe length, and height that will make these measurements consistent for all measurers. (Fig. 2.16 shows students measuring stride length.)

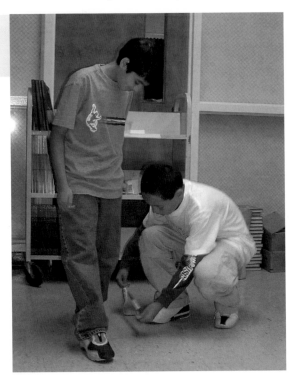

Fig. **2.16.**

Students measure their stride lengths.

Before the students arrive on the scene of the crime, complete some additional preparations. Collect several yardsticks or tape measures and tape them to the wall to create stations where students can easily measure their heights. Tape others to the floor to make stations where students can readily measure their shoe lengths and stride lengths. Then use flip-chart paper (or transparencies) to set up two T-charts with space for data on every student in the class. In one, the column headings should be "Shoe Length" and "Height," and in the other, they should be "Stride Length" and "Height."

Engage

When your students come to class and find your staged "crime scene," they will want to know what's going on. Tell them that a crime—a theft—occurred during the night. Say what was taken, indicate its value to you, and explain that the thief made the shoeprints on the floor and is still at large. One teacher happened to receive a bag of microwavable kettle corn as a present from a student on the day when he was planning to stage the crime scene. The gift of the kettle corn shaped the scenario that the teacher then developed. His story to his students ran as follows:

Last night, a shocking crime was committed in this classroom! A bag of delicious kettle corn, given to me only yester-

Navigating through Mathematical Connections in Grades 6–8

day as a gift, was stolen! If this item is not recovered, I have little hope of having anything to snack on later in the week. Please help me find the person who took the kettle corn. My expectation of snack-time pleasure and, indeed, my general mental well-being are at stake! Can the evidence at the crime scene help you learn anything about our criminal so that you can solve this mystery and restore the kettle corn to your distraught teacher?

Create your own story, with suitable embellishments, to engage your students in the work of solving the crime.

Explore

Assign your students to groups of four. Have them discuss, first in their groups and then as a class, what they could learn about the thief from the evidence of the footprints in the flour. Your students may offer various ideas, including identifying the type of shoe that the criminal wore or determining whether the size or type of shoe indicates that the criminal is male or female.

On their own, students may suggest the idea of using the shoe length or stride length to predict the height of the criminal. If brainstorming does not produce suggestions about two possible relationships—shoe length to height, and stride length to height—introduce them into the conversation yourself. You might ask, for example, "Does the evidence in the flour provide any clues? Could you measure any attributes of the criminal? What measurements could you make *directly*? Could these measurements help you make any other measurements *indirectly*?"

Give each group of four students a copy of the blackline master "Who Committed the Crime?" Direct the students' attention to step 1, which asks what measurements someone could obtain directly from the evidence at the scene. The students' suggestions should include shoe length and stride length; they may mention the area of the shoeprint, as well.

Take this opportunity to measure both the thief's shoe length and his or her stride length while your students watch. Alternatively, you could ask a student to make these measurements for the class. (If you do so, be sure to select someone whom you trust to exercise care and not mess up the evidence.) Obtaining one reliable set of measurements for all the students to use later is likely to be a better approach than having each group obtain its own measurements. With many measurements, the evidence might soon be smeared or even obliterated. An additional advantage to making the measurements while the students look on is that this process provides an opportunity to discuss possible techniques to increase consistency and reliability among measurements. Post the measurements that you obtain for the thief's shoe length and stride length for all the students to see and record in step 1 on their activity sheets.

In steps 2 and 3, the students should speculate that each of these measurements might serve as a predictor of the thief's height. Ask the students how they can test their conjectures. What data can they collect and analyze to determine, for example, whether there is a relationship between shoe length and height? On their own, students might suggest finding the measurement of every person's shoe length and height in the class, and then finding the ratio of height to shoe length, or shoe length to height, for each person. If the ratios are all roughly the same, the students will have an empirical basis for believing that height and shoe length are in fact related. Some students may even suggest finding the average shoe length and the average height and then finding their ratio.

If your students have had experience with graphing, they may suggest creating a scatterplot or graph as a way to represent all the data and look for trends. A scatterplot offers a good visual representation of the relationship between two measurements. Students who have completed the investigation have usually preferred scatterplots over other types of data displays.

Give each group of students two sheets of centimeter grid paper and have the groups complete steps 4–6, which ask them to collect and display their data. Using the tape measures or yardsticks that you have set up in the room, the students measure shoe length, stride length and height for each member of their groups, enter the measurements into T-charts on their activity sheets, and transfer them to the class T-charts that you set up in advance.

Each group then uses the grid paper to make two scatterplots of the data displayed in the class T-charts. Check to see if they label the axes correctly in their scatterplots. (Students can use graphing calculators to plot the data if you prefer.)

The axes in the students' scatterplots should of course be "Shoe Length" and "Height" in one plot, and "Stride Length" and "Height" in the other. In the interest of consistency and easy comparisons, have the students label their axes in the same way. *Height* is the unknown variable in the case of the thief, so have your students show "Height" on the y-axis in both plots, and "Shoe Length" on the x-axis in one plot and "Stride Length" on the x-axis in the other.

Once students have made their scatterplots, they must decide whether the data in each plot show a linear trend, which they can use to predict the height of the criminal. In classrooms where students have conducted the investigation, they have usually found that both graphs show linear trends (although several classes' data demonstrated a linear trend in only one of the scatterplots).

In a scatterplot that shows a linear trend, the data points cluster in such a way that most of them are close to a line that can be drawn through them. When data points are widely spread, or it is not clear that they line up in any way, the data may not demonstrate a linear trend. Or they may demonstrate a linear trend that is very weak, and a line may not be the best model for describing the relationship. If your class includes students whose heights are quite varied, the data are more likely to demonstrate clear linear trends. If your students are similar in height, the data will not spread out as much. In this case, you might try to get measurements from some other people (faculty, older or younger students, and so on).

If the data show a linear trend, the students can try to find the *line of best fit* for the data set. This is the line that minimizes the sum of the squares of the distances between all the points and the line itself. Students can experiment to decide where they think the line falls by placing a length of uncooked spaghetti or a clear ruler on the plot.

NCTM's Illuminations Web site offers several explorations involving models of linear data in different settings. Consider using these to extend your students' understanding of linear relationships. See http:// illuminations.nctm.org/ LessonDetail.aspx?id=L298.

A well-placed line will have points above and below it, as well as some points on it. Students often believe they should place the line so that it passes through as many points as possible. Be sure to correct this misconception. Explain that it is important that about half the points be on or above the line and half be on or below the graph.

Students who are using a graphing calculator have two ways of identifying the line of best fit. They can have the graphing calculator perform a linear regression and produce the line of best fit electronically. However, using a guess-and-check approach can give the students a richer experience with the calculator. They can enter an equation that they think might yield the line and then adjust the equation until the line falls where they think it should. As they enter different equations and inspect their graphs, they can assess the equations' similarities and differences. For example, students comparing the equations $y = 2x + 41$ and $y = (1.9)x + 42$ as possible models for the relationship of shoe length to height can describe the second equation as slightly "flatter" or "less steep" than the first. They can also readily see that the y-value of the point at which the first equation crosses the y-axis ($y = 41$) is 1 less than the y-value of the point at which the second equation crosses the y-axis ($y = 42$). This approach gives students an excellent opportunity to understand the impact of m and b in the equation $y = mx + b$.

In one classroom, students noticed that for every inch of change in the shoe length, the change in the height was approximately two inches. By subtracting $2x$ from the y values, they noticed a difference of about 41 or 42, resulting in the rules for the two sample scatterplots from students shown in fig. 2.17.

When the groups determine their lines of best fit, they are likely to discover that the lines vary somewhat. Each group should then try to

Students who do not have access to graphing calculators can experiment with the applet Changing Slope and y-Intercept, which appears on the accompanying CD-ROM. This interactive applet offers a dynamic demonstration of the impact of changes in m (slope) and b (y-intercept) on the graph of a linear function. It is important that students understand the relationships between the symbolic and graphical representations of a function.

Fig. 2.17.

Two samples of scatterplots from students, graphing height against shoe length

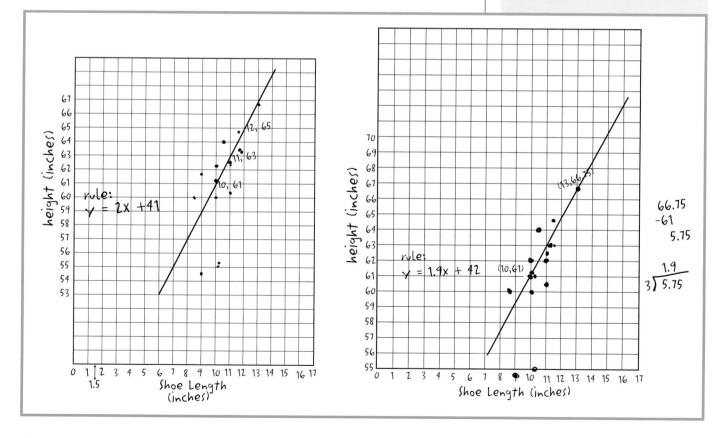

Understanding that the line of best fit represents a linear function that describes data helps students make an important connection between algebra and data analysis. Experiences with patterns and data help them understand *change* as a fundamental mathematical concept.

Students collect data and analyze a scatterplot to determine whether a linear relationship exists between height and shoe length or between height and stride length. If they find such a relationship, they can also find an equation that will serve as a mathematical model that they can use to predict a person's height from his or her stride length or from his or her shoe size.

write the equation for its line. It can be helpful for the groups to share their equations and for the class to discuss whether the equations are reasonable.

The equation that the students write for the line is a mathematical model of the relationship between the two variables. Be sure that your students understand this idea. It is important for them to see that the numerical measurements, the scatterplot, and the equation give them three representations—numerical, graphical, and symbolic—of the same data.

As students create these representations, they should see the advantages of each. The table offers quick access to the exact data, but the graph is a much easier way to see if there is a linear trend. Once the students have determined that the data show a linear trend, they can find an approximate line of best fit. The equation of this line gives them a model that they can easily use to make predictions based on data.

Explain

Steps 7 and 8 on the activity sheet ask the students for their conclusions. Do their data indicate that a relationship exists between an attribute that they can measure directly (the thief's shoe length or stride length) and an attribute that they cannot measure directly (the thief's height)? If so, they must describe the relationship in words and symbols, and then they must say whether they think they can use the relationship to predict the unknown attribute for the thief.

Understanding that the line of best fit represents the linear function that most accurately describes the collected data allows students to make an important connection between algebra and data analysis. Too often when students explore linearity, they work with data that actually *are* linear. Such experiences do not adequately prepare them for real-world data, which are not usually so neat. The students' discovery that they can find a linear function that provides a reasonable description of "untidy" data can significantly advance their mathematical understanding. The experience of collecting "messy," authentic data, creating a scatterplot, and finding the line of best fit can be a highly effective way for students to see that a linear function can offer the best description of a relationship in data.

Step 9, the last step on the activity sheet, asks the students to use the information that the line of best fit has given them to make a prediction about the height of the criminal. Each group can apply their equations or graphs to determine how tall they think the thief is, and students can record this prediction on the activity sheet.

Evaluate

If your selected "criminal" is one of your students, include him or her in a group of four or five other students that you call on to appear at the front of the classroom in a "police lineup." If your thief is a fellow teacher or an administrator at your school, arrange for a small group of school staff members to come to your classroom and form a lineup. Make sure the heights of your selected suspects are significantly different from one another. Have each suspect write his or her height boldly on a sheet of paper and hold it up for students to see.

Have each student write down his or her conclusion about the criminal's identity. Tell the students to support their conclusions with

Navigating through Mathematical Connections in Grades 6–8

evidence. Once all the students have selected their suspects and given their reasons for their choices, call on the "real" thief to to open his or her backpack, jacket, or whatever hiding place you and your assistant agreed on, revealing the stolen item.

Extend

Students can explore other attributes of the shoeprints in the flour. For example, they can find the area of the prints and the area of the soles of their own shoes and see if the area of a shoeprint is a predictor of a person's height. Could they have used shoeprint area, as well as shoe length and stride length, to identify the guilty party?

Students could also extend their work by investigating relationships between shoe length and height, or stride length and height, in samples from different populations. Would the data show a linear trend if the subjects were all adults or if they were very mixed in age? Students could bring in measurements of shoe length and height, or stride length and height, for family members or friends and see if the trends are the same as in their class data or different.

Students can also extend their understanding by discussing similarities and differences among the lines of best fit that they found and determining which of these lines they think is the best predictor of height.

In the class of the teacher who alleged that his package of kettle corn had been stolen, the students concluded that a shoe length of 12 inches predicts a height of about 65 or 66 inches. At this moment, a teacher who was about 66 inches tall walked by, eating popcorn. A few students noticed her in the hall and called out, "Mrs. Klino did it!" The "thief" was thus successfully unmasked.

This lively activity has been used effectively in a variety of contexts—even a "mathematics night" for families. The investigation involves students actively in meaningful mathematics while providing a brief and fairly simple glimpse of applications of mathematics in investigations of crimes. The students gain firsthand experience of some the mathematical processes that criminologists use to follow clues and develop profiles, thus narrowing the field of suspects and helping them answer the ever intriguing question, "Who did it?"

How Many Fish in the Pond?

Goals

- Experiment with the idea of using a sample to analyze a population

- Explore the mathematics of the sampling technique known as capture-recapture

- Use a sampling activity to support proportional reasoning skills

- Develop algebraic thinking, including the ability to recognize and use patterns in problem solving

Materials and Equipment

For each workstation serving four or five students—

- A 2- or 3-quart plastic bowl (or a sturdy flat-bottomed paper bag or a wide-mouthed jar)

- Approximately 300 counters (fish-shaped crackers or dried beans or other small objects that can be easily tagged with a marking pen)

- One or two marking pens, in colors that will show up on the counters

- A small cup for scooping "fish" (a small yogurt container, for example)

- A spoon or other implement for mixing the counters

For each group of four students—

- A copy of the blackline master "Fishing for Data"

For each student—

- A copy of the blackline master "Reeling In an Estimate"

pp. 145–46; 147–49

Learning Environment

The students work in groups of four at workstations that the teacher has set up in advance around the classroom. They gather data on samples of "fish" from a population in a "pond." After they have collected their data, they work either collaboratively or independently, as the teacher prefers, to investigate the mathematics of the capture-recapture method of sampling.

Prior Knowledge or Experience

- Experience in using data to make estimates

- Familiarity with the use of a survey to describe characteristics of a sample

- Flexibility in representing numbers and understanding ratios, including percentages

- Experience in working with patterns and generalizing them to make predictions

Overview

The students estimate the total number of "fish" (fish-shaped crackers, dried beans, or other counters) in a "pond" (a bowl, paper bag, or jar) by using the *capture-recapture* sampling method employed by wildlife specialists and ecologists to estimate the size of a closed population (Nichols 1992). Working in groups of four, the students capture fish from the pond. They mark each fish in this initial "capture," count them, record the total, and return them to the pond, mixing them with the unmarked fish. They then recapture fish, sampling the fish population that is now composed of marked and unmarked fish. They consider whether the ratio of marked fish to total fish in a typical "recapture" sample would be equivalent to the ratio of marked fish to total fish in the pond. They use this proportional relationship, along with a modification of it designed to reduce error, to arrive at two estimates of the population of fish in the pond. They check their estimates by counting the actual number of fish in the pond, and they calculate the percentage difference between the actual total and each of their estimates.

By exploring this sampling technique, the students see the usefulness of mathematical methods in answering a complex question, and they "use [a] mathematical model to represent and understand [a] quantitative relationship" (NCTM 2000, p. 222). This achievement is one of the goals of the Algebra Standard, as outlined in *Principles and Standards for School Mathematics*. The students develop other important algebraic thinking skills as well, including the ability to recognize relationships among patterns and to make connections to the symbolic representations of algebraic situations.

The investigation also reinforces the students' understanding of "ways of representing numbers [and] relationships among numbers" and strengthens their abilities to "compute fluently and make reasonable estimates," as emphasized by the Number and Operations Standard (NCTM 2000, p. 214). Moreover, the students develop their understanding of fundamental concepts of measurement, as they "apply appropriate techniques, tools, and formulas to determine [a] measurement" and solve a problem by "using ratio and proportion," as the Measurement Standard suggests (NCTM 2000, p. 240).

In addition, sampling exposes the students to important processes and applications of data analysis. They work with a "question that can be addressed with data and collect [and] organize ... relevant data to answer" it, and they "develop and evaluate inferences and predictions that are based on data," as the Data Analysis and Probability Standard recommends (NCTM 2000, p. 248).

Finally, the activity supports the students' facility with the processes as well as the content of mathematics. It reinforces their problem-solving skills by giving them a problem that they can solve by "apply[ing] ... a variety of appropriate strategies," as outlined in the Problem Solving Standard (NCTM 2000, p. 402).

Discussion

How many fish are in the North Sea? How many birds are in South America? These types of questions are frequently asked but do not have exact answers because of the difficulty of counting every fish or bird.

A closed population is one that no individuals leave (by death or emigration) or enter (by birth or immigration) during the time that a sampling survey is under way. The definition is thus quite restrictive, and many field situations are likely to violate it.

What if we change these questions slightly and ask instead, "How many fish are in this pond?" and, "How many birds nest in this park?" These changes help make the questions answerable by restricting the areas in question and thus the populations under consideration.

Even so, answering such questions is challenging. How would we go about counting the fish in a pond or the deer in a forest? On the one hand, if wildlife biologists report that 40 elk live in Smokey Mountain National Park, we suppose that someone went out into the park and counted them. On the other hand, if we learn that 10,000 buffalo roam the plains at Little Bighorn National Park, we are unlikely to imagine that we are getting an exact count. We assume that the large round number is an estimate and that the biologists or mathematicians who came up with it used some other way of counting besides the conventional method of matching each item in a set consecutively with a counting number.

An important part of environmental biology is determining the size of animal populations. Conservation scientists often need to know the size of a species' population in a given area to make important decisions about wildlife management. However, these populations are often too large or scattered to count directly. Scientists have to find alternative ways to count the populations of certain species in particular habitats. Some of these methods include *sampling*, *direct observation*, and *indirect observation*. One especially useful sampling technique is called *capture-recapture*.

Scientists using the capture-recapture technique capture some of the animals in a population, tag or mark them in some way, count them, and then let them go free in the original population. After giving the animals time to mingle and mix once again with that population, the scientists again capture animals from the population. In this new capture (called a *recapture*), the scientists are likely to find many animals that they did not mark the first time. If their sample is large enough, however, they are also likely to find some animals that they did mark.

If the number of marked animals in a recapture is not zero, the scientists can use the ratio of marked animals to total animals in the recapture to estimate the number of animals in the whole population. To increase the reliability of the recapture ratio, scientists typically conduct multiple recaptures and average the data. As described in more detail below, they reason that the ratio of marked animals to unmarked animals in the recapture should, in theory, be equal to the ratio of the number of animals that they originally marked to the number of animals in the whole population. Thus, scientists can make a reasonable estimate of the size of a population of animals in the given area.

Engage

Ask your students, "How could you count all the fish in a pond?" Engage them in a discussion of this question. Encourage them to think about difficulties associated with counting whole populations. Ask them to consider how they would determine the number of students in their class, their school, the state, the nation, and the world. Students will realize that large populations are impossible to count exactly; mathematical models are often necessary to provide reasonable estimates.

Navigating through Mathematical Connections in Grades 6–8

Sometimes the size of the population is not the only impediment to making an exact count. Practical considerations can intervene as well. The students should agree that they could not take all of the fish out of the pond and count them without potentially harming or destroying fish. Thus, they would need an alternative method of counting the fish.

If your students do not suggest the idea of sampling to arrive at a reasonable estimate of the number of fish in a pond, suggest the concept yourself by introducing an example from another real-world context. Say, "When people want to know the opinions of a large number of people, sometimes they gather opinions from a relatively small number of people. They use the data from this small sample to draw conclusions about the whole population of interest. Do you think you could use a similar strategy to count the fish in the pond?" Be sure that your students understand the difference between *sample* and *population*.

Explore

Tell your students about the development of the capture-recapture technique of estimating the size of a closed population. The strategy is not new. John Graunt first used it in 1662 to estimate the population of the city of London. Later, in 1896, C. G. J. Petersen used the technique again to estimate the harvestable stocks of Danish fish populations. In 1930, F. C. Lincoln of the U.S. Fish and Wildlife Service also employed the technique to estimate waterfowl abundance in flyways of the United States.

The capture-recapture technique (two-sample, closed-population model) is in fact sometimes called the Lincoln-Petersen model. Although the terminology may make the procedure sound complicated, its mathematics, as the students discover, is quite straightforward and simple.

Explain to your students that they are going to experiment with the capture-recapture sampling technique, which they will use to estimate the size of a population. Assign the students to groups of four, and give each group a single copy of the blackline master "Fishing for Data." Send each group to a workstation that you have set up in the classroom. Each station should have a bowl of fish crackers, dried beans, or other counters to represent a pond teeming with fish. Each station should also have two or three marking pens, a spoon or other implement for mixing the fish, and a small cup for the students to use in recapturing fish.

Tell the students to follow the steps on the sheet to collect data that they will then use to estimate the population of "fish" in the "pond." They should select one student in the group to "fish" in the pond, two people to mark and count captured fish, and one student to serve as the record keeper for the group. If possible, space the workstations so that the groups can work independently without getting in one another's way.

As the students collect data from their samples, they will begin to see the mathematics behind the capture-recapture method of arriving at a population estimate. They will use symbols to represent numbers in meaningful ways. The activity will help them become accustomed to using N to stand for the total number of individuals in the population.

The students draw a sample of M fish from the population. They mark these fish (with colored dots on both sides), count them, and

Population refers to the whole set of individuals whose number or characteristics are of interest in answering a complex question. *Sample* refers to a small set of individuals drawn from the population in question to supply data that will accurately represent the larger set.

 "Census 2000 and Sampling" (Yamada 2000; available on the CD-ROM) provides an excellent development of the process of sampling.

In practical terms, in many wildlife surveys N is the total population of a selected animal species *in a particular region* or the size of the "catchable" population.

"release" them back into the population. They then mix the marked and unmarked fish, simulating the natural mixing and mingling that occur over time in a "real" capture-recapture procedure as the tagged animals disperse and distribute themselves in the population.

Next, the students capture a sample of n fish from the same population. This sample, called a "recapture," must be large enough to be likely to include marked animals from the original capture. The students count the marked fish in this sample, denoting their number by m. The activity sheet directs the students to gather data from ten recapture samples.

When all the groups have collected their data, give each student a copy of the second activity sheet, "Reeling In an Estimate." Each student transfers the group's data to his or her own sheet. This sheet offers guidance in using the data to explore the mathematics of the capture-recapture method. Your students can continue to work in their groups on the sheet, or you can ask them to work by themselves. Be sure that your students clearly understand that—

- N stands for the number of fish in the population;
- M stands for the number of fish that were originally captured and marked;
- n stands for the number of fish in the recapture;
- m stands for the number of marked fish in the recapture.

Discuss why the first activity sheet, "Fishing for Data," asked the students to make ten recapture trials. Why does the new activity sheet, "Reeling In an Estimate," ask them to find *average* values for n and m from the ten trials?

As your students work with the mathematics on the new sheet, help them understand that an animal's chance of being in the recapture does not depend on whether or not it was in the original capture. Therefore, in theory, the proportion of marked animals in the second sample is equivalent to the proportion of marked animals in the total population:

$$\frac{M}{N} = \frac{m}{n}.$$

Solving for N yields a population estimate known as the Lincoln index:

$$N = \frac{nM}{m}.$$

Discuss what happens if the size of the recapture sample is small. In such a case, the above estimate is *biased*, or prone to error. For example, suppose that in a small sample the number of marked animals, or "recaptures" (m), is zero? Chapman showed that when the recapture sample is small, the Lincoln index of population size is biased. The bias in an estimate based on a small sample can significantly affect its accuracy.

To underscore the point, ask the class to consider the problems associated with sampling only a small number of students to determine how all the students in a school view a particular issue. A survey of a larger number of students would be more likely to capture the actual ideas.

In 1951, D. G. Chapman developed a modified version of the Lincoln-Petersen technique to reduce bias in the population estimate. Chapman's estimate of population size, denoted as N_C, adds in a "correcting factor" (+ 1), which increases the accuracy of the model. N_C can be computed as follows:

$$N_C + 1 = \frac{(n+1)(M+1)}{m+1}$$

$$N_C = \frac{(n+1)(M+1)}{m+1} - 1.$$

This formula is a simplified expression, appropriate for middle school students. Actual sampling applications may use other, more complex models.

The capture-recapture method for estimating a population rests on a number of assumptions. As discussed earlier, first among these is the supposition that the population of interest is *closed*. Different techniques exist for working with an *open* population, although geographical isolation is still essential. Open-population techniques are often used in studies that continue over an extended period of time.

Explain

Using the formulas for the Lincoln index and the Chapman population estimate, the students determine two estimates of the number of "fish" in the "pond." They then make an actual count of the fish—something that wildlife and environmental specialists ordinarily cannot do. Having a countable population allows the students to make useful comparisons between the actual N and each of their estimates, thus evaluating the accuracy of the estimates.

To make these comparisons, the students find the percentage difference between the actual population and each estimate that they obtained with data from the capture-recapture method. The students use the following formula to find the percentage difference:

$$\% \text{ difference} = \frac{(\text{larger number}) - (\text{smaller number})}{\text{average of the two numbers}} \times 100$$

For example, if the original population was 300 and an estimate was 250, the percentage difference would be

$$\% \text{ difference} = \frac{300 - 250}{275} \times 100 = \frac{50}{275} \times 100 = \frac{200}{11} = 18.18\%.$$

To help your students understand how and why the formula works, ask questions such as the following:

- "Why do you subtract the smaller number from the larger one?" (To measure the absolute difference between the two counts—actual and estimate)
- "Why do you average the two numbers?" (In this case, comparing the absolute difference to either the actual count or the estimate doesn't really make sense. The students are not trying to find a percentage that compares the difference to an "old" number that they had "first," as they would if someone said, "Yesterday, I had $100, and today I have $120. What is the percentage increase in my money?" In that case, the students would compare the difference, $20, to the original amount, $100, for an increase of 20 percent. By contrast, in the case of

A population may be closed for geographic reasons—for example, all of its members may live in a lake instead of a river—or for demographic reasons. An open *population is a population that changes in size and composition as a result of births, deaths, and movement. Encourage your students to consider these descriptors when considering sampling populations.*

the actual population and the estimate, the difference between the two numbers has no "directionality." Consequently, the students need to find a point of comparison that is different from either number. The midpoint between the two numbers is a reasonable point of comparison. Averaging gives the point midway between the actual count and the estimate.)

- "Why do you divide the difference between the two numbers by the average of the two?" (To show the difference between actual count and the estimate as a fraction of the number that is midway between the two)
- "Why do you multiply your result by 100?" (To convert the fraction to a percentage)

Have students explain the meaning of the percentage differences that they have calculated in the context at hand. In a whole-group discussion, ask—

- "What constitutes a 'large' percentage difference in our situation with the fish in the pond?" (Let students compare results with one another. The Solutions section presents the results of two class-room experiments; see pp. 169–170. The Chapman population estimates that these students determined on the basis of their data were not very close to the actual population of 300. The percentage differences were 32 percent and 59 percent and would definitely be considered "large.")
- "What do you suppose could cause a 'large' percentage difference?" (A small sample)
- "How do you think you might modify the investigation to ensure a smaller percentage difference?" (Enlarge the sample size)

Evaluate

Sampling is an important statistical concept. Middle school students can develop a basic understanding of some of the important principles related to sampling techniques (see also Meader and Storer [2000]). This activity provides the teacher with an opportunity to listen to students' discussions about sampling and ask questions that will provide feedback about their understanding.

One primary concept that students should understand is the difference between populations and samples. Ask questions and initiate discussions that help students differentiate between these terms.

One way to extend this understanding is to have students identify populations and samples in a variety of contexts. Say, for example, "Consider the students in your school as a population under study. What might be some samples of this population?" Students might suggest males, seventh graders, students in a particular corridor of the school, or every twentieth student selected from the school roster. Ask, "Would all of these samples be of equal value in a survey of the school's student population?"

Emphasize that the purpose of sampling is to represent the population of interest. Engage students in conversations about whether the samples they identified represent the population of all the students in their school. How could they select samples that would give a better picture of all students?

Navigating through Mathematical Connections in Grades 6–8

As you evaluate your students' progress on the activity, pay attention to both how the students work with the formulas and how they interpret the results. The investigation gives students a valuable opportunity to formulate questions and draw inferences from data. To maximize their learning, they should focus not only on the procedures for sampling but also on the underlying statistical concepts.

Extend

To extend your students' experience with sampling to estimate an animal population, you might introduce one or two alternate forms of animal population survey. *Transect sampling* and *quadrat sampling* are two techniques your students might investigate.

Transect sampling involves counting or otherwise measuring specimens along a transect to survey the abundance or distribution of organisms in a natural environment. A transect is a narrow, continuous strip in which someone makes observations or measurements to draw inferences about a population of interest. Someone walks a line from point *A* to point *B*, gathering data from the sample of the population within a defined area on either side of the line. In general, a transect survey draws data from multiple transects.

Transect sampling often seeks a correlation (match) between the distribution of organisms and other environmental factors. For example, the reduced distribution of a particular plant might correlate with increasing soil salinity.

In most transect sampling, the width of the band within which a person counts individuals of a species of interest should remain constant. This consistency is especially important if data from one transect will be compared directly with data from another. In general, the distance from the path should be as great as possible, to maximize information, but not so great that the members of a population of interest cannot be seen or heard along the transect. Someone using transect sampling to survey a population of birds might count all the birds that he sees or hears within a twenty-meter band on either side of a one-kilometer route in a thirty-minute period.

Keeping the length and width of a transect consistent from transect to transect makes estimating a population easier in the long run. Nevertheless, one can survey a population effectively by using transects of different lengths and widths. Landscapes can be very different from one survey site to the next, and it is sometimes difficult to select a distance that is workable in every situation. Certain landscapes and situations may warrant the use of a broader or narrower band.

There are ways to account for different widths when attempting to make comparisons among sites. A transect of any width can work. As for length, if one kilometer is too long, the distance can be shortened in 100-meter decrements. Someone who wants to cover more than one kilometer can collect data on two transects—one whose length is one kilometer, and the other whose length is the remaining distance beyond one kilometer. The important thing is to determine the width and length of each transect at the start of a survey. Changing the size of a transect in the middle of a monitoring effort would bias the data, and the resulting error would have to be accounted for in final analyses.

Quadrat sampling is another method of estimating the abundance or density of a population of interest by sectioning a habitat and survey-

A *transect* is a narrow, continuous strip in which someone makes observations or measurements to draw inferences about a population of interest. In a transect survey of a wildlife population, a transect serves as the sample area.

A *quadrat* is a square (or rectangle, circle, or other shape)
of a set size that is placed as a
frame or otherwise marked out in
the habitat of a population under
study. In a quadrat survey, a
quadrat is the sample area.

ing a percentage of the sections. A quadrat is a square (or rectangle, circle, or other shape) of a set size that is placed as a frame or otherwise marked out in the habitat of the population under study. The quadrat is thus the sample area in quadrat sampling. A number of quadrats are selected, with wildlife specialists identifying and recording the specimens of interest in each one. Sometimes researchers carefully sort through the organisms on site, and sometimes they photograph each quadrat and analyze the organisms later.

Both transect sampling and quadrat sampling use a number of mathematical formulas that your students can examine. If A_T stands for the total area (*length* $\times$ *width*) of the habitat in which the population of interest lives, and A_S stands for the total area sampled,

$$A_S = \frac{\% \text{ area sampled}}{100} \times A_T.$$

The area of a transect (A_t) or a quadrat (A_q) is equal to its length times its width (if the quadrat is rectangular). A_t times the number of transects, or A_q times the number of quadrats, is thus equal to the total area sampled, or A_S.

Once your students have considered both methods, you can ask them to compare and contrast the two, focusing on when these methods are valid and when they are not. Lead a class discussion in which you pose such questions as the following:

- "Why might someone need transect or quadrat sampling methods?" (Quadrat and transect surveys are both passive sampling methods; that is, they do not involve capturing or removing individuals from their habitats. These types of surveys can be very useful in situations where it is important to gather information on biodiversity or abundance without disturbing wildlife in a natural setting.)

- "How are the two methods similar? How are they different?" (In both methods of passive sampling, wildlife experts delineate particular tracts as regions in which to sample individuals in a population of interest in a larger area that is also well defined. The two kinds of surveys use different types of areas to sample a population, as well as different techniques for collecting data. A transect is a strip that cuts through the region in which the population of interest lives, and a wildlife specialist typically traverses the strip while counting the individual specimens of this population. A quadrat is usually an area marked off by a frame or fence within the region in which the population of interest lives, and a specialist systematically examines every square unit of the quadrat while counting the individuals in it.)

- "How do these methods differ from the capture-recapture method of estimating the size of a population?" (Neither transect sampling nor quadrat sampling involves capturing individuals in a population of interest.)

Students could explore these methods by finding and reporting on interesting examples of each type of survey posted on the Internet. For

Navigating through Mathematical Connections in Grades 6–8

example, they can locate information about using quadrat sampling to investigate the diversity of marine life at

http://www.coml.org/edu/tech/count/quadsamp-p1.htm,

and an account of the use of transect surveys to estimate the abundance of manatees in an island region of Southwest Florida at

http://sofia.usgs.gov/geer/2003/posters/aerialsurvey/.

Conclusion

Chapter 2 has presented a group of activities that show ways to help students discover and understand the connections between the ideas and processes of mathematics and the content of numerous other disciplines. Not only does mathematics touch these other areas but lends them vital support, making solutions possible to a host of complex problems.

Be sure that your students understand that many more fields rely on mathematics than are represented in the seven investigations in this chapter. The investigations here hardly begin to hint at the variety and richness of the mathematical applications and models that scientists, engineers, architects, doctors, and a myriad of other specialists use every day.

Nevertheless, these activities and others like them can play valuable roles in the mathematics education of middle school students, giving them glimpses of mathematics that is often hidden in the methods of other disciplines—buried, though it is hard at work behind the scenes. Your students' understanding and appreciation of mathematics can grow when you bring this buried mathematics to the fore, showing it for what it is and unfolding its indispensable contributions to spectacular achievements in many different arenas of today's world.

NAVIGATIONS SERIES

GRADES 6–8

NAVIGATING *through* MATHEMATICAL CONNECTIONS

Looking Back and Looking Ahead

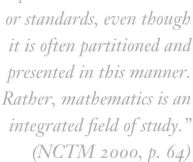

"Mathematics is not a collection of separate strands or standards, even though it is often partitioned and presented in this manner. Rather, mathematics is an integrated field of study."
(NCTM 2000, p. 64)

Middle-grades students too often encounter mathematics as a collection of separate topics with little apparent application to the real world. By contrast, instruction that emphasizes connections can provide students with important experiences that help them explore, develop, and expand their understanding of the interconnectedness of mathematical topics and the interrelatedness of mathematics and other disciplines. As *Principles and Standards for School Mathematics* (NCTM 2000) asserts, "Teachers can facilitate these connections in several ways: They should spotlight the many situations in which young students encounter mathematics in and out of school. They should make explicit the connections between and among the mathematics ideas students are developing" (p. 132).

Students who experience a curriculum that emphasizes this connectedness develop an understanding of the usefulness of mathematics and its relationship to everyday situations. The activities in this book help students see connections among mathematical concepts and between mathematics and other pursuits in the real world. The investigations challenge you to continue to reflect on how to emphasize connections in your teaching.

Children begin school with many perceptions about how mathematics is embedded in their world. Their daily activities often contextualize mathematics. Concepts of number and shape are rooted in their experiences and environment. Children recognize and use mathematics in their daily lives.

As children explore relationships among different mathematical concepts and topics, their mathematical investigations become more

"The teacher's role includes selecting problems that connect mathematical ideas within topics and across the curriculum; it also includes helping students build on their current mathematical ideas to develop new ideas."

(NCTM 2000, p. 277)

"Teachers need to take special initiatives to find ... integrative problems when instructional materials focus largely on content areas and when curricular arrangements separate the study of content areas such as geometry, algebra, and statistics. Even when curricula offer problems that cut across traditional content boundaries, teachers will need to develop expertise in making mathematical connections and in helping students develop their own capacity for doing so."

(NCTM 2000, p. 359)

sophisticated. Their awareness of the interrelationships among concepts serves as a bridge between their conceptual and procedural understanding, giving them a solid foundation on which to build mathematical knowledge and skill as they grow.

In the middle grades, students begin to study mathematical concepts that are increasingly abstract. Seeing connections among these ideas is a powerful way of developing an appreciation for the usefulness of mathematical inquiry. Students should have opportunities to explore problems and use multiple approaches and ideas to reach solutions. Throughout these experiences, you should make explicit efforts to build on your students' previous mathematical understanding to help them grasp new ideas.

When mathematics instruction emphasizes connections, students' understanding of relationships increases, as does their ability to apply them. Recognizing connections is an important mathematical process. Students need to be skillful in making meaningful associations among concepts and between concepts and procedures. When students at the secondary level encounter the same or related mathematical concepts in multiple contexts, in problems that they can solve with different strategies or representations, they should recognize the interconnectedness of the ideas as well as the connections between the ideas and the processes that they use in working with them.

As students encounter mathematical ideas in other disciplines and in the real world, they should be able to use and extend connections that they have discovered among mathematical concepts, applying them in other disciplines. As they move toward careers or further academic studies, they should take with them a deep appreciation for connections that will expand as they study more sophisticated mathematics.

Mathematical modeling is an important way to emphasize connections and is the primary approach used in this book. In the middle grades, a strong mathematics curriculum that relies on modeling promotes an understanding of connections and prepares students for more advanced studies in mathematics. It can give them skills that they begin to use immediately and later extend as their understanding and appreciation of mathematics grows in work settings and everyday life. Seeing connections builds the mathematical reasoning skills that make mathematics a powerful tool and students effective problem solvers.

GRADES 6–8

NAVIGATING *through* MATHEMATICAL CONNECTIONS

Appendix

Blackline Masters and Solutions

Pyramid Scheme?

Name_____

Ritzville Experiments—Part 1

In the eastern part of the state of Washington, many farmers grow wheat. When they produce a surplus, they often store their unsold wheat in huge outdoor piles, which they cover with large pieces of heavy-duty vinyl to protect them from wind, snow, and rain. Motorists driving on Interstate 90 near the small community of Ritzville come on an immense storage area with many vinyl-covered stacks of wheat. Some travelers have described the enormous stacks rising from the rolling plains as "pyramids." In fact, the stacks have been called the "Ritzville pyramids."

1. Consider what a pyramid is.

   a. Give a definition of *pyramid*.

   b. Do you suppose that the term *pyramid* is mathematically correct for the shape of such a pile of wheat?

   c. If not, what mathematical term would you use to describe the shape that you would expect a very large pile of wheat to have?

2. Investigate your ideas about the shape of a Ritzville pyramid.

   a. Line a fairly flat pan (such as a pie plate or a pizza pan) with a paper towel.

   b. *Very slowly* pour one cup of rice to form a pile on the paper towel.

c. Make a drawing of your pile of rice from a vantage point directly above it.	*d.* Draw a side view of your pile of rice.

The activity Ritzville Experiments is adapted from Nowlin, Donald, "Practical Geometry Problems: The Case of the Ritzville Pyramids," *Mathematics Teacher* 86 (March 1993): 198–200.

Name_____

3. *Very slowly* add another cup of rice to your pile of rice.

a. Draw your new pile of rice from a point directly above it.	*b.* Draw a side view of your new pile of rice.

4. *Very slowly* add the third cup of rice to your pile of rice.

a. Draw your new pile of rice from a point directly above it.	*b.* Draw a side view of your new pile of rice.

5. What mathematical shape is your pile of rice beginning to take? _____

   Is this the shape that you expected it to have? _____ Explain.

Ritzville Reflections

Name_____

Ritzville Experiments—Part 2

Suppose you are a farmer in Ritzville, Washington, and you have stacked your unsold wheat in an enormous pile whose shape is shown in the diagram.

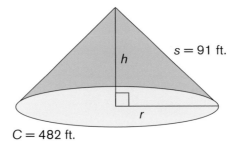

Imagine that your pile of wheat has already been covered with heavy-duty protective vinyl for storage, but you want to know how much vinyl the covering used. You can easily walk around your stack and measure its *circumference*, C. In addition, the vinyl helps stabilize your pile of wheat, allowing you to measure the stack's *slant height*, s, directly. Note, however, that you cannot make direct measurements of either the height, h, of the stack or the radius, r, of its circular base.

Suppose that you measure the slant height of your pile of wheat as 91 feet and the circumference as 482 feet (making both measurements to the nearest foot).

1. What would you need to measure to find the amount of vinyl in the covering on your pile of wheat? (Don't try to make the measurement now—just say what you would need to measure to solve the problem!)

2. Suppose that for an inventory at the storage area you must declare the amount of wheat in your stack. What would you need to measure to find the amount? (Again, don't try to make the measurement now—just say what you would need to measure to solve the problem!)

_____

The activity Ritzville Experiments is adapted from Nowlin, Donald, "Practical Geometry Problems: The Case of the Ritzville Pyramids," *Mathematics Teacher* 86 (March 1993): 198–200.

Sizing Up a Cylinder

Name_____

Ritzville Experiments—Part 3

If you needed to measure the vinyl on your stack of unsold wheat in Ritzville, Washington, you might begin by thinking about the *net* of the geometric solid formed by the stack. A net is a two-dimensional pattern of a three-dimensional solid. It can be folded or curved to form the solid. Before investigating the net for your Ritzville stack, explore the net of a simpler solid—a cylinder. Farmers store other crops besides wheat in open areas. You have probably seen large cylindrical rolls of hay lying out in fields. Experiment with a cylindrical object, such as a soup-can label or a paper-towel core. Each is a cylinder without bases.

1. If you made a net of a soup-can label or paper-towel core, what shape do you think it would have?

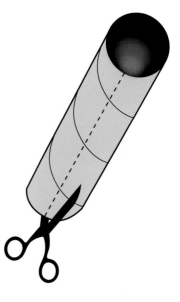

2. Cut your cylinder from edge to edge, as in the diagram, making the *shortest cut* that you can.

3. Open your cut cylinder and spread it flat, forming the net of the *lateral surface* of the cylinder. What shape is it? _____ Make a sketch.

4. Suppose that you wanted to make bases to complete a net for a cylinder.

    a. How could you determine what size they should be? (Don't actually make the bases—just say how you would go about making them.)

    b. Where do you think you would place the bases in relation to the net of the lateral surface to form the net of the cylinder? Make a sketch, and explain your placement of the bases.

The activity Ritzville Experiments is adapted from Nowlin, Donald, "Practical Geometry Problems: The Case of the Ritzville Pyramids," *Mathematics Teacher* 86 (March 1993): 198–200.

Name_____

5. Consider a different cylinder (with bases this time). Carefully complete the following tasks in any order:

   a. Use paper (or cardstock), tape, and scissors to create a model of your cylinder.

b. Draw a side view of your cylinder below. (Your drawing need not be full size or precisely to scale.)	c. Draw the net of your cylinder. (Your net need not be full sized or precisely to scale.)

6. Using colored pens or pencils, add color-coordinated labels on the three items (model, side view, and net) that you created in step 5, identifying the following elements:

   a. The cylinder's lateral surface

   b. The cylinder's bases

   c. The circumferences of the cylinder's bases

   Use one color to show each element on all three items. In the appropriate color, add any sketches or explanatory comments that you think are helpful.

7. a. In the net of your cylinder, where did you need to place the bases in relation to the cylinder's lateral surface?

   b. Is this what you expected?

Conic Considerations

Name_____

Ritzville Experiments—Part 4

Your discoveries in part 3 ("Sizing Up a Cylinder") have brought you closer to measuring the vinyl on your stack of surplus wheat in Ritzville, Washington. The next step is to investigate the net of a cone. Experiment with a pointed party hat. Such a hat is a cone without a base.

1. *a.* If you made a net of a cone without a base, what shape do you suppose it would have?

   b. Make a sketch to show your idea.

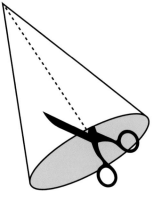

2. To test your conjecture in step 1, cut your party hat from bottom to top, as shown in the diagram, making the *shortest cut* that you can.

   The cut that you are making is along the *slant height* (*s*) of the cone. The point at the top is called the *apex*.

3. Open your cut party hat and spread it flat, forming the net of the *lateral surface* of a cone.

   a. Describe the shape of this part of the net of a cone.

   b. Does this shape match the shape that you drew in 1(*b*)? _____ Explain.

4. Suppose that you wanted to cut out a base to complete a net for the cone.

   a. How could you determine what size it would be? (Don't actually make the base—just say how you would go about making it.)

The activity Ritzville Experiments is adapted from Nowlin, Donald, "Practical Geometry Problems: The Case of the Ritzville Pyramids," *Mathematics Teacher* 86 (March 1993): 198–200..

Name_____

b. Where do you think you would place the base in relation to the net of the lateral surface to form the net for the cone? Make a sketch, and explain your placement of the base.

5. Consider a different cone (complete with a base this time). Carefully complete the following tasks in any order:

a. Using paper (or cardstock), tape, and scissors, create a model of your cone.

b. Draw a side view of your cone below. (Your drawing need not be full size or precisely to scale.)	c. Draw the net of your cone. (Your net need not be full sized or precisely to scale.)

6. Using colored pens or pencils, add color-coordinated labels on the three items (model, side view, net) that you created in step 4, identifying the following elements:

a. The cone's lateral surface

b. The cone's base

c. The slant height of the cone's lateral surface

d. The circumference of the cone's base

Use one color to show each element on all three items. In the appropriate color, add any sketches or explanatory comments that you think are helpful.

7. In the net of your cone, where did you need to place the base in relation to the cone's lateral surface?

Completing the Circle

Name_____

Ritzville Experiments–Part 5

How can your discoveries about the net of a cone help you measure the area of the vinyl on your stack of wheat in Ritzville, Washington? Experiment with two paper plates (or other equal-sized disks) to find out.

1. Both you and your partner have been assigned an angle measurement. Record the measurements below.

   a. My angle measurement _____

   b. My partner's angle measurement _____

   Note that together the measurements of the angles equal 360 degrees.

2. Using just one disk, a protractor, and a straightedge, carefully measure either your angle or your partner's as a *central angle* of the disk. (A central angle has its vertex at the center of a circle, so you must first find the center of the disk.)

3. Cut out the sector of the circle defined by the angle. Use a pen or pencil to record the angle measurement directly on the sector. Because your angle measurement and your partner's sum to 360 degrees, you now have sectors that represent both of your angle measurements. Record the other angle measurement on the second sector.

4. Compare each sector with your uncut disk, lining up the sector's straight edges with radii of the circle. The curved part of a sector is called the *circumference of the sector*. It would be the circumference of the base of the cone that you could make from the sector—but don't make the cone yet!

   a. Do you suppose that your angle measurement helps you determine the fraction of the circumference of the whole circle that the circumference of your sector represents?

   b. Do you suppose that your angle measurement helps you determine the fraction of the area of the whole circle that the area of a sector represents?

5. Measure the circumference of your sector and your partner's by using a string that you can then measure in centimeters.

   a. Circumference of my sector ≈ _____ cm

   b. Circumference of my partner's sector ≈ _____ cm

_____

The activity Ritzville Experiments is adapted from Nowlin, Donald, "Practical Geometry Problems: The Case of the Ritzville Pyramids," *Mathematics Teacher* 86 (March 1993): 198–200..

Name_____

6. Measure the area of your sector and your partner's by tracing each sector's outline on a piece of centimeter grid paper (or several pieces taped together, if necessary) and counting squares.

   a. Area of my sector ≈ _____ cm^2

   b. Area of my partner's sector ≈ _____ cm^2

7. Calculate the circumference and area of your uncut disk by applying familiar formulas.

   a. Using the formula $C = 2\pi r$ and either $\frac{22}{7}$ or 3.14 as an approximation for π, calculate the circumference of your circle.

   C_{circle} _____

   b. Using the formula $A = \pi r^2$ and either $\frac{22}{7}$ or 3.14 as an approximation for π, calculate the area of your circle.

   A_{circle} _____ cm^2

8. Express the circumference of each of your sectors as a fraction of the circumference of the whole circle.

   a. $\dfrac{C_{sector}}{C_{circle}}$ for my sector _____

   b. $\dfrac{C_{sector}}{C_{circle}}$ for my partner's sector _____

9. Express the area of each of your sectors as a fraction of the area of the whole circle.

   a. $\dfrac{A_{sector}}{A_{circle}}$ for my sector _____

   b. $\dfrac{A_{sector}}{A_{circle}}$ for my partner's sector _____

10. Consider the following claim about two ratios—the *area of a sector* to the *area of the whole circle*, and the *circumference of the sector* to the *circumference of the whole circle*:

    For any sector of a circle and the circle itself, $\dfrac{\text{Area of sector}}{\text{Area of circle}} = \dfrac{\text{Circumference of sector}}{\text{Circumference of circle}}$.

    Do you think this claim is true or false? _____ Explain.

11. Keep your uncut disk, your two sectors, and your data for use in part 6—"Developing the Data."

Developing the Data

Name_____

Ritzville Experiments–Part 6

If it is true that for any sector of a circle and the circle itself,

$$\frac{Area\ of\ sector}{Area\ of\ circle} = \frac{Circumference\ of\ sector}{Circumference\ of\ circle},$$

you will have a proportional relationship that can help you find the area of the vinyl on your Ritzville stack of wheat. But does this relationship hold? The following steps will let you investigate by gathering and analyzing data.

1. In part 5 ("Completing the Circle"), you and your partner cut two sectors with particular central angles from a given circle. Then you measured the circumference of each of your sectors with a string and the area of each sector by counting squares on grid paper.

   a. In columns 3 and 5 of the chart below, enter your measurements of these circumferences and areas in the respective rows for your angle measurements.

   b. What fraction of 360° (the central angle of a full circle) is the central angle of each of your sectors? Compute the fractions, and enter them in column 2 in the respective rows.

   c. Gather data from your classmates to complete columns 2, 3, and 5 in the chart below. When you are finished with this step, your chart should show the circumferences and areas of all the sectors in your class's experiment.

(1) Angle measurement (degrees)	(2) Fraction of a circle	(3) Circumference of the sector (C_{sector}) in the experiment (cm)	(4) Ratio $\frac{C_{sector}}{C_{circle}}$	(5) Area of the sector (A_{sector}) in the experiment (cm²)	(6) Ratio $\frac{A_{sector}}{A_{circle}}$
30°					
45°					
60°					
90°					
120°					
135°					
150°					
180°					
210°					
225°					
240°					
270°					
300°					
315°					
330°					

The activity Ritzville Experiments is adapted from Nowlin, Donald, "Practical Geometry Problems: The Case of the Ritzville Pyramids," *Mathematics Teacher* 86 (March 1993): 198–200.

Name_____

2. *a.* Working with a calculator, compute the ratios $\dfrac{C_{sector}}{C_{circle}}$ and $\dfrac{A_{sector}}{A_{circle}}$ for all the sectors represented by central angle measurements in your chart.

   b. Enter your results in columns 4 and 6 of your chart.

3. For each sector represented in your chart, compare your data in columns 2, 4, and 6.

   a. What do you observe?

   b. Do your data appear to support the claim above about the equality of the ratios? _____ Explain.

4. Using what you have discovered about the ratios, determine the circumference and area of your sector and your partner's sector again, this time with mathematics.

   a. Calculate the circumference of your sector and your partner's as a fraction of the circumference of the whole circle. (You can use your calculation of the circumference of the circle in step 7[*a*] of part 5.)

   Circumference of my sector ≈ _____ cm

   Circumference of my partner's sector ≈ _____ cm

   b. Calculate the area of your sector and your partner's as a fraction of the area of the whole circle. (You can use your calculation of the area of the circle in step 7[*b*] of part 5.)

   Area of my sector ≈ _____ cm²

   Area of my partner's sector ≈ _____ cm²

5. How do your calculations in step 4 compare with the measurements that you obtained in steps 5 and 6 of part 5?

6. Carefully make cones from your sector and your partner's sector by taping the radial (straight) edges together *with no overlap.* Set your cones aside for use in part 9 ("Can You Be More Precise?").

Coming to the Surface

Name_____

Ritzville Experiments—Part 7

Your experimental data in part 6 suggest that for any cone

$$\frac{C_{sector}}{C_{circle}} = \frac{A_{sector}}{A_{circle}}.$$

With this proportional relationship, can you find the surface area of your stack of wheat in Ritzville, Washington, with just the two measurements that you have, *without knowing the central angle of the sector?* Experiment to find out.

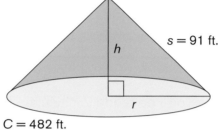

s = 91 ft.

C = 482 ft.

Assume as before that you measured the circumference (*C*) of your stack as 482 feet and the slant height (*s*) as 91 feet, making both measurements to the nearest foot.

1. You need to measure the area of the vinyl on your stack. You know that this area is the lateral surface area of the cone that your stack forms. You also know that the net of the lateral surface of your stack is a sector of a circle.

    a. Make a *rough* sketch of this sector. (Obviously, you can't show its central angle accurately, but your sketch can still be useful for organizing information.)

    b. Label two measurements in your sketch: *C* and *s*. For clarity, give *C* as C_{sector}.

2. The sector in your sketch shows the lateral surface area of your stack. Label this area as A_{sector}. What units will your measurement of A_{sector} have?

The activity Ritzville Experiments is adapted from Nowlin, Donald, "Practical Geometry Problems: The Case of the Ritzville Pyramids,"
Mathematics Teacher 86 (March 1993): 198–200..

Name_____

3. In your sketch, complete the circle to which the sector belongs, and label its circumference as C_{circle}.

Your experiments have shown you that $\dfrac{C_{sector}}{C_{circle}} = \dfrac{A_{sector}}{A_{circle}}$. Multiplying both sides of the equation by A_{circle} gives

$$\frac{C_{sector}}{C_{circle}} \times A_{circle} = A_{sector}.$$

Remember from your experiments that $\dfrac{C_{sector}}{C_{circle}}$ is equal to the fraction of 360° that the central angle of the sector represents. So, without knowing the central angle of the sector used to form your cone, you can use the equation $\dfrac{C_{sector}}{C_{circle}} \times A_{circle} = A_{sector}$ to find A_{sector}. You have a value for C_{sector} (see your sketch). If you can find values for C_{circle} and A_{circle}, then you'll be ready to calculate the value of A_{sector}, the area of the vinyl on your stack of wheat in Ritzville, Washington.

4. Determine C_{circle}, the circumference of the full circle, by using the familiar formula $C = 2\pi r$. (You know that the radius of the full circle is s, the slant height of the cone. Don't use an approximation for π this time. Simply give your answer in terms of π, and remember to show your measurement's units.)

$C_{circle} \approx$ _____

5. Determine A_{circle}, the area of the full circle, by using the familiar formula $A = \pi r^2$. (Don't use an approximation for π here, either. Simply give your answer in terms of π, and remember to give your measurement's units.)

$A_{circle} \approx$ _____

6. Substitute the values for C_{sector}, C_{circle}, and A_{circle} into $\dfrac{C_{sector}}{C_{circle}} \times A_{circle} = A_{sector}$, and calculate A_{sector} (note that you can cancel out π in the calculation). Be sure to give the units for your measurement of A_{sector}.

Note that your measurement of the vinyl uses rounded values. As a result, it is less exact than its significant digits suggest. Rounding to the hundreds place can give a value closer to the true value. Note also that because a sheet of vinyl with this area covers your stack with no overlap, this area is the minimum amount of vinyl needed to cover the stack. As a farmer storing unsold wheat in Ritzville, you would certainly expect your stack to be securely covered, so the storage facility would be likely to round up still more.

Volumes Yet to Learn!

Name_____

Ritzville Experiments—Part 8

You now know how much heavy-duty vinyl the storage facility in Ritzville needed to cover your stack of wheat. However, for an inventory at the facility, you still must declare the amount of wheat in your stack.

1. What would you need to measure this time? (Refer to your answer in part 2 if it is available.)

2. What type of units would you use to measure this quantity? _____ Why?

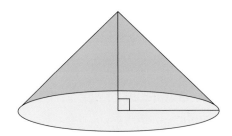

The activity Ritzville Experiments is adapted from Nowlin, Donald, "Practical Geometry Problems: The Case of the Ritzville Pyramids," *Mathematics Teacher* 86 (March 1993): 198–200.

Can You Be More Precise?

Name_____

Ritzville Experiments—Part 9

Before trying to determine the volume of your Ritzville stack of wheat, experiment again with rice, as in part 1 ("Pyramid Scheme?"). Explore the volumes of two sample cones by using different techniques for measuring rice in them.

1. If you are working with the same partner that you had in part 5 ("Completing the Circle"), you and your partner can use your original pair of cones. Label your cones A and B. If you have a new partner, make new cones A and B as your teacher directs.

2. Remember that the net of the lateral surface of a cone is a sector of a circle. The lateral surfaces of cones A and B are sectors of the *same* circle, and together they compose the area of that circle. What fraction of the area of the circle does each of the sectors represent?

   a. The sector for cone A represents _____ of the area of the circle.

   b. The sector for cone B represents _____ of the area of the circle.

3. In part 8 ("Volumes Yet to Learn!"), what type of unit did you conclude that you would need to measure the quantity of wheat in your stack? _____ (You will need this type of unit here to measure the rice in a cone.)

4. Suppose that cones identical to A and B are filled with rice, and you and your partner want to estimate how much rice is in each by determining how many "cubes of rice" each of your cones will hold. You intend to obtain two sets of estimates by measuring the volumes of your cones with different-sized cubes of rice. You will measure each cone with larger cubes of rice (2 cm on an edge) and smaller cubes of rice (1 cm on an edge). Use the following process to make cubes of rice:

   a. Using a straightedge calibrated in centimeters and a piece of cardstock or paper, *carefully* make nets for two rectangular prisms—a cube that is 2 centimeters on an edge and a cube that is 1 centimeter on a edge.

   b. Using scissors, cut out each net, fold it, and tape it together to form a "box" with an open "lid."

   c. Pour rice into each cube until it is level with the top.

   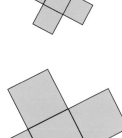

5. In cubic centimeters, how much rice does each cube hold?

   a. Amount of rice in the cube that is 1 cm on an edge _____ cm³

   b. Amount of rice in the cube that is 2 cm on an edge _____ cm³

The activity Ritzville Experiments is adapted from Nowlin, Donald, "Practical Geometry Problems: The Case of the Ritzville Pyramids," *Mathematics Teacher* 86 (March 1993): 198–200..

Can You Be More Precise? (continued)

Name_____

6. To verify your response in 5(*a*), carefully pour the rice from your smaller cube (1 cm on an edge) into a small graduated cylinder.

   a. According to the gauge on the cylinder, how much rice is in the smaller cube?

   b. Is this measurement in the units that you used to report your response in 5(*a*)?

   c. If not, how does this measurement compare with your response in 5(*a*)?

   d. Adjust your response in 5(*a*) if necessary, and then pour the rice from the cylinder back into your original container of rice.

7. To verify your response in 5(*b*), carefully pour the rice from your larger cube (2 cm on an edge) into the small graduated cylinder.

   a. According to the gauge on the cylinder, how much rice is in the larger cube? _____

   b. How does this measurement compare with your response in 5(*b*)?

   Adjust your response in 5(*b*) if necessary, and then pour the rice from the cylinder back into your original container of rice.

8. Now you can use plastic cubes (1 cm on an edge or 2 cm on an edge) in place of actual cubes of rice to estimate the volume of rice that each of your cones will hold. The chart below will help you organize your work. Complete column 2 by entering the fractions for cones A and B from step 2.

(1)	(2) Fraction of the circle	(3) Number (N) of cubes (2×2×2 cm) needed to fill cone	(4) Amount of rice in N cubes (cm³)	(5) Number (M) of cubes (1×1×1 cm) needed to fill cone	(6) Amount of rice in M cubes (cm³)	(7) Amount of rice needed to fill cone directly (cm³)
Cone A						
Cone B						

9. Start with plastic cubes that are 2 centimeters on an edge. Fill your cones, one at a time, with these cubes.

   a. How many cubes do you need? (The students in your class should reach an agreement on how to handle any cubes that "stick out over the top.") Enter the numbers in column 3 of the chart.

Name_____

  b. In 5(*b*), you recorded the amount of rice in a cube that is 2 centimeters on an edge. Use this information to complete column 4 in the chart. These entries will give you your first estimates of the amount of rice that each of your cones will hold.

10. Now measure with plastic cubes that are 1 centimeter on an edge. Fill your cones, one at a time, with these cubes.

  a. How many cubes do you need? Enter the respective numbers in column 5 of the chart.

  b. In 5(*a*), you recorded the amount of rice in a cube that is 1 centimeter on an edge. Use this information to complete column 6 in the chart. These entries will give you a second set of estimates of the amount of rice that each of your cones will hold.

11. Compare your estimates in column 4 with your estimates in column 6. What observations can you make?

12. Now fill your cones directly with rice. When the rice is level with the top of a cone, pour it carefully into a large graduated cylinder to measure.

  a. How much rice was in each of your cones? (Depending on the size of your cones, you may have to measure your rice in stages, filling the cylinder and then emptying it before measuring remaining amounts of rice.)

  b. Enter the amounts (in cm^3) in column 7 to complete the chart in step 8.

13. Examine all three amounts that you have entered in your chart as the volume of rice in each cone.

  a. How do your three sets of measurements compare in size?

Name_____

b. How can you explain the variation in your three estimates of the volume of each cone?

c. Which estimate do you think gives the *most precise* measurement of the volume of each cone?

_____ Why is this measurement more precise than either of the others?

d. Which estimate do you think gives the *least precise* measurement of the volume of each cone?

_____ Why is this measurement less precise than either of the others?

e. Can you suggest any way of making an even more precise measurement of the volume of one of your cones?

Turning Up the Volume

Name_____

Ritzville Experiments—Part 10

In part 9 ("Can You Be More Precise?"), you used three methods to estimate the volumes of two cones. Now consult with your classmates, and use the following chart to compile your results and theirs. Which of your cones has the greatest volume?

A	B	C	D	E	F
Fraction of the circle	Number (N) of cubes (2×2×2 cm³) needed to fill cone	Amount of rice in N cubes (cm³)	Number (M) of cubes (1×1×1 cm³) needed to fill cone	Amount of rice in M cubes (cm³)	Amount of rice needed to fill cone directly (cm³)
$\frac{1}{12}$					
$\frac{1}{8}$					
$\frac{1}{6}$					
$\frac{1}{4}$					
$\frac{1}{3}$					
$\frac{3}{8}$					
$\frac{5}{12}$					
$\frac{1}{2}$					
$\frac{7}{12}$					
$\frac{5}{8}$					
$\frac{2}{3}$					
$\frac{3}{4}$					
$\frac{5}{6}$					
$\frac{7}{8}$					
$\frac{11}{12}$					

The activity Ritzville Experiments is adapted from Nowlin, Donald, "Practical Geometry Problems: The Case of the Ritzville Pyramids," *Mathematics Teacher* 86 (March 1993): 198–200.

Navigating through Mathematical Connections in Grades 6–8

Turning Up the Volume (continued)

Name_____

1. For each cone in the chart, you should have three estimates of volume. On grid paper, make a graph.

   a. Let the *x*-axis in your graph show the fractions of the circle that the lateral surfaces of the cones represent. Label your *x*-axis "Fraction of the Circle." Be sure that your scale accurately represents the proportional relationships among the fractions!

   b. Let the *y*-axis in your graph show measurements of volume. Label your *y*-axis "Volume (cm^3)."

   c. Use three colored pens or pencils for your measurements of volume on your graph. Select one color for the measurements obtained with the cubes that are 2 centimeters on an edge (column C), a second color for the measurements obtained with the cubes that are 1 centimeter on an edge (column E), and a third color for the measurements obtained by pouring rice directly into the cones (column F).

   d. Do you think you should you connect the "dots" for each colored set of measurements in your graph? _____ Why, or why not?

2. For each cone, you have shown three measurements of volume on your graph. Compare the three sets of measurements with one another.

   a. Which measurement technique do you think has given the most precise measurements?

   _____ Why?

   b. Is this conclusion consistent with your results in step 13 of part 9 ("Can You Be More Precise?")

   _____

3. By examining your chart, identify the cone that has the greatest volume.

   a. What fraction of the circle does this cone's lateral surface represent?

   b. What central angle did someone cut from the circle to make this cone?

   c. What central angle of the circle remained?

4. Did you expect so much variation in the volumes of the cones? _____ Explain.

A Second Look at Cylinders

Name_____

Ritzville Experiments—Part 11

In parts 9 and 10, you made your most precise measurements of the volume of a cone by filling it directly with rice, which you then measured. By extending your data, you can discover a little "inside information" that will help you obtain the volume of a cone *mathematically* instead of *experimentally.*

1. As you learned in part 3 ("Sizing Up a Cylinder"), farmers store hay as well as wheat outdoors. The volume of a cylinder of hay is simpler to determine than the volume of a cone of wheat, just as the surface area of a cylinder was easier for you to evaluate than the surface area of a cone.

   a. Draw a cylinder, and label the radius of its base as *r* and its height as *h*.

   b. The volume of a cylinder is the area of the base times the height:

   $$V_{cylinder} = \pi r^2 h$$

   Does the formula for the volume of a cylinder make sense to you? _____ Explain. (*Hint:* Compare the formula for the volume of a cylinder with the formula for the volume of a rectangular prism: $V = l \times w \times h$).

2. Choose one of the two cones (cone A or cone B) that you and your partner worked with in part 9 ("Can You Be More Precise?").

   a. What is your cone's slant height?

   $s \approx$ _____ cm

   b. What is your cone's circumference?

   $C \approx$ _____ cm

The activity Ritzville Experiments is adapted from Nowlin, Donald, "Practical Geometry Problems: The Case of the Ritzville Pyramids," *Mathematics Teacher* 86 (March 1993): 198–200.

Name_____

c. Use the familiar formula $C = 2\pi r$ to find the radius of your cone's base. (Use $\frac{22}{7}$ or 3.14 as an approximation for π.)

$r \approx$ _____ cm

d. Suppose that the diagram below shows the right triangle formed by the height, h, the radius, r, and the slant height, s, of your cone. From the Pythagorean theorem, you know that $r^2 + h^2 = s^2$.

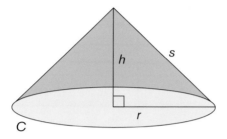

Substitute your values for s and r, and determine h, the height of your cone.

$h \approx$ _____ cm

3. Imagine that you have a cylinder whose base has the same radius, r, as that of your cone and whose height, h, is the same as that of your cone.

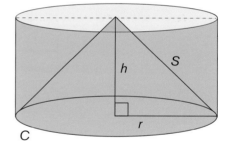

a. Use the formula $V_{cylinder} = \pi r^2 h$, with $\frac{22}{7}$ or 3.14 as an approximation for π, and determine the volume of such a cylinder.

$V_{cylinder} \approx$ _____ cm³

b. Examine the chart that you completed in step 8 in part 9 ("Can You Be More Precise?"). Find the measurement that you obtained for the volume of your cone by filling it directly with rice. Enter that value here.

$V_{cone} \approx$ _____ cm³

A Second Look at Cylinders (continued)

Name_____

c. What is the ratio of the volume of your cone to the volume that you calculated for the cylinder with the same height and same radius for the base? (Use a calculator and give a decimal value.)

4. a. Consider your cone as cone 1 in the chart below, and enter the results of your work in 3(a), (b), and (c) in row 1:

Cone	V_{cone} (cm³)	$V_{cylinder}$ (cm³)	$\dfrac{V_{cone}}{V_{cylinder}}$
1			
2			
3			
4			
5			
6			
7			
8			
9			
10			

b. Complete the chart by collecting data on nine other cones from your classmates.

5. Examine the ratios in column 4 of your chart.

a. Are the ratios similar to one another? _____ Explain.

b. Are the ratios consistently close to a common fraction? _____ Explain.

c. Can you make a conjecture about a formula for the volume of a cone?

V_{cone} = _____

Navigating through Mathematical Connections in Grades 6–8

A Value for the Volume

Name_____

Ritzville Experiments–Part 12

Your experiment in part 11 demonstrated empirically that the volume of a cone is $\frac{1}{3}$ of the volume of a cylinder with the same base and height:

$$V_{cone} = \frac{1}{3}\pi r^2 h.$$

With this formula, you are set to use mathematics to find the volume of your stack of wheat in Ritzville, Washington.

1. Assuming as before that you measured the slant height (s) of your pile of wheat as 91 feet and its circumference (C) as 482 feet (making both measurements to the nearest foot), what units do you think your measurement of the volume of wheat will have?

2. A diagram of your stack appears below.

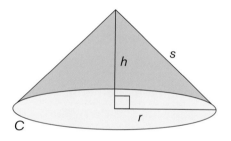

a. Substitute your measurement for C into the familiar formula $C = 2\pi r$, and solve for r, the radius of your conical stack of wheat. (Use $\frac{22}{7}$ or 3.14 as an approximation for π, and round your measurement to the nearest foot.)

$r \approx$ _____ ft.

b. Note that the diagram above shows the right triangle formed by the height, h, the radius, r, and the slant height, s, of your stack. From the Pythagorean theorem, you know that $r^2 + h^2 = s^2$. Substitute your measurement for s and the value that you just calculated for r, and solve for h, the height of your conical stack. (Round your measurement to the nearest foot.)

$h \approx$ _____ ft.

The activity Ritzville Experiments is adapted from Nowlin, Donald, "Practical Geometry Problems: The Case of the Ritzville Pyramids," *Mathematics Teacher* 86 (March 1993): 198–200..

Name_____

3. *a.* Substitute your values for *h* and *r* into the formula for the volume of a cone. Determine how much wheat is in your Ritzville stack. (Use $\frac{22}{7}$ or 3.14 as an approximation for π, and round your measurement to the nearest cubic foot. Be sure to label the units in your measurement!)

$V \approx$ _____

    b. Do the units in your measurement here match your idea in step 1?

    c. Because your calculations use rounded measurements, your results contain error. Round to the thousands place for a value that is closer to the true value.

4. Suppose that the storage facility in Ritzville requires that you declare the quantity of wheat in your stack in *bushels* (bu).

    a. Use your rounded value from 2(*c*) and the equivalence 1 bu $\approx$ 1.25 ft^3, and give the volume of your stack in bushels.

    You have now solved both Ritzville problems, encountering many related mathematical ideas along the way!

Name_____

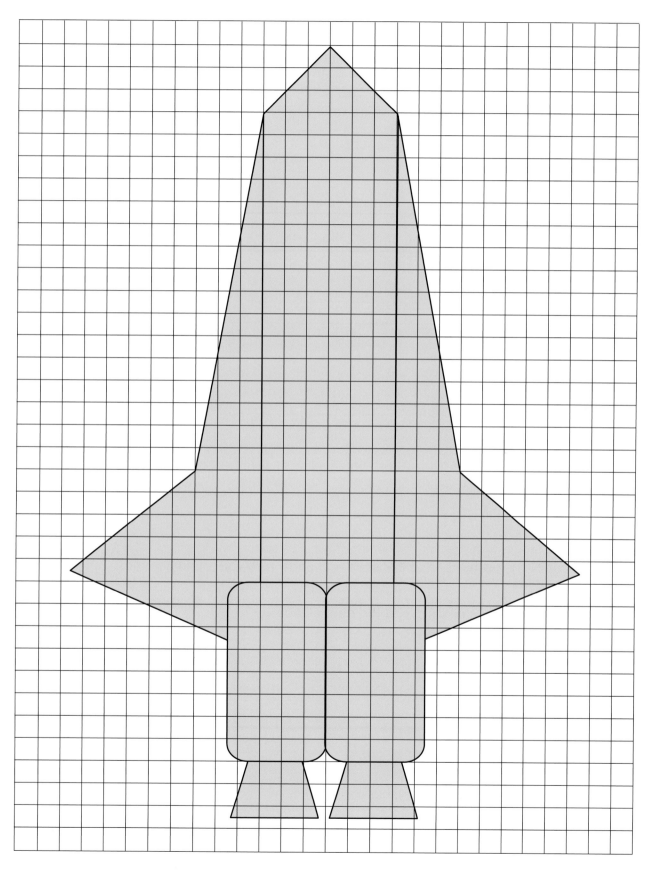

Sizing the Silhouette

Name_____

Refer to the activity page "Shuttle Silhouette" in responding to the following questions:

1. In linear grid units, what is the perimeter of the silhouette of the shuttle?

2. Mark the outline of the shuttle to show how you found its perimeter.

3. Explain in words how you found the perimeter of the silhouette of the shuttle. Is your answer exact or approximate?

4. In square grid units, what is the area of the silhouette of the shuttle?

5. Draw on the outlined cross section of the shuttle to show how you found its area.

6. Explain in words how you found the area of the cross section of the shuttle. Is your answer exact or approximate?

This activity is adapted from Borasi, Raffaella, and Judith Fonzi, *Professional Development That Supports School Mathematics Reform* (Arlington, Va.: National Science Foundation, 2002).

Dinosaur Scaling

Name_____

1. The drawing above shows the skeleton of a dinosaur known as Anchisaurus. Working with a scale of 1 cm : 14 cm (size shown to actual size), complete the table on the next page by determining scaled-down and "real-life" measurements for the Anchisaurus.

   • Technically, the *length of the body* is the distance from the shoulder blades to the pelvic bone.

   • Likewise, the *depth of the body* is the longest part of the rib cage.

   • The *femur* is the upper leg bone; the *tibia* is the larger lower leg bone.

   • The *humeris* is the upper arm bone; the *radius* is the larger bone in the lower arm.

2. A process called *elastic scaling* provides a more realistic picture by taking into account the variation in the density of the bones in an animal's skeleton. Elastic scaling makes an adjustment in the regular scale factor for length when it is applied to the diameter of a weight-bearing bone. The regular scale factor for length does not take account of the extra thickness of the bones that support large amounts of weight in animals. Zoologists have found that raising the scale factor for length to the $\frac{3}{2}$ power gives a more accurate indication of the diameters of weight-bearing bones. For example, if the scale factor is 1 : 9, then elastic scaling would raise 9 to the $\frac{3}{2}$ power, giving 1 : 27 in the case of the 1 diameter of a weight-bearing bone. These bones would include the femur, the tibia, the humerus, the radius, and the tail.

Dinosaur Scaling (continued)

Name_____

Attribute	Measurement in Scale Drawing (cm)	Measurement in Real Life (cm)	Attribute	Measurement in Scale Drawing (cm)	Measurement in Real Life (cm)
Total Length			Length of Head		
Hip Height			Width of Head		
Length of Body			Length of Humerus		
Depth of Body			Diameter of Humerus		
Length of Femur			Length of Radius		
Diameter of Femur			Diameter of Radius		
Length of Tibia			Length of Tail		
Diameter of Tibia			Tail Diameter at Body		

a. Look again at the data for the Anchisaurus in the table. Determine the elastic scale on the basis of the 1 : 14 scale that you used.

b. Using your elastic scale from 2(a), reestimate the real-life diameters of the following support bones in the skeleton of the Anchisaurus:

Femur _____   Tibia _____   Tail _____

Humerus _____   Radius _____

c. Why does it make sense to use a different scale for the diameters of these bones? How do the revised diameters of these scaled bones support your reasoning?

Digging *Holes*

Name_____

In the Newbery-winning novel *Holes* by Louis Sachar, teenager Stanley Yelnats has been sentenced to eighteen months' labor at Camp Green Lake, a spartan detention center where delinquent boys dig holes all day in a dry lakebed under the scorching Texas sun. Every day, including Saturdays and Sundays, Stanley must dig a hole that is as deep and as wide as the five-foot shovel that he is issued for the task: "The shovels were five feet long, from the tip of the steel blade to the end of the wooden shaft. Stanley's hole would have to be as deep as his shovel, and he'd have to be able to lay the shovel flat across the bottom in any direction" (p. 27).

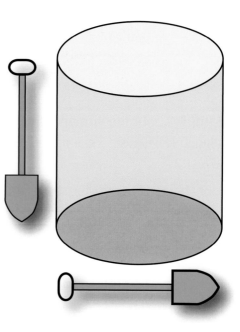

One of the boys, X-Ray, always claims a particular shovel: "They all looked the same to Stanley, although X-Ray had his own special shovel, which no one else was allowed to use. X-Ray claimed it was shorter than the others, but if it was, it was only by a fraction of an inch" (p. 27).

Suppose that X-Ray's shovel is actually a full half-inch shorter than all the others. What difference would this make in his day's work?

1. Think about a hole dug by Stanley with a five-foot shovel and a hole dug by X-Ray with a shovel that is shorter by half an inch. Do you think there would be much of a difference in the quantities of dirt that the two boy removed to make the holes? If so, about how much of a difference do you think there would be? (Give your answer in cubic inches or cubic feet.)

2. On a separate piece of paper, use a compass to draw one circle that is 5 inches in diameter and another circle that is 4.5 inches in diameter. Find the area of each circle. What is the difference in the areas of the two circles? _____

3. What did you discover in creating and comparing your two circles?

_____

This activity draws on the novel *Holes* by Louis Sachar (New York: Farrar, Straus and Giroux, 1998).

Digging *Holes* (continued)

Name______________________________________

4. Would you like to change your answer in step 1 to reflect what you learned in comparing the two circles? ______________ If so, record a revised estimate in the space below.

5. Think about the size and shape of Stanley's and X-Ray's holes. On a separate piece of paper, sketch each hole, label its dimensions, and find the amount of dirt that each boy would remove in one day.

6. By taking the shorter shovel, how much dirt would X-Ray avoid having to remove from his hole in one day? ________________________

7. Design a box that would hold the additional dirt that Stanley would remove from his hole but that X-Ray would not have to remove from his. Draw a picture below that shows the dimensions and explain how you found your answer.

8. Look again at your estimate in step 1 (or in step 4 if you revised the estimate). Do you think your estimate was reasonable? _____________ Explain.

9. What do you think is a reasonable size for the error in an answer to this problem?

Getting the *Holes* Picture

Name_____

In "Digging *Holes*," you figured out how much dirt Stanley Yelnats and his cabin-mate X-Ray would remove from their holes in one day, with Stanley using a 5-foot shovel and X-Ray using a shovel that is shorter by half an inch. In Louis Sachar's novel *Holes*, the first hole is hard, but not the hardest, and the boys dig many holes—one a day, day in and day out. "After a while … [Stanley] lost track of the day of the week, and how many holes he'd dug. It all seemed like one big hole, and it would take a year and a half to dig it" (p. 59).

Assume that the Stanley and X-Ray dig holes every day, with no days off. They work through the weekends and on holidays. Explore what would happen over time if they continued to dig holes with shovels of unequal length.

1. Complete the tables below to show how much dirt (in cubic feet) Stanley and X-Ray would remove in one week, two weeks, three weeks, and so on.

Stanley

Number of Weeks	Dirt Removed (ft³)

X-Ray

Number of Weeks	Dirt Removed (ft³)

2. *a.* Explain in words how you would find the dirt that each boy would remove in a certain number of weeks at Camp Green Lake.

This activity draws on the novel *Holes* by Louis Sachar (New York: Farrar, Straus and Giroux, 1998).

Name_____

b. Using numbers and symbols, write a rule for the amount of dirt that Stanley would have removed by the end of any given week.

c. Write a rule for the amount of dirt that X-Ray would have removed by the end of any given week.

3. Write a rule that you could use to determine the difference in the dirt that the boys would have removed in a given number of weeks at Camp Green Lake.

4. Suppose that X-Ray and Stanley both ended up staying at Camp Green Lake for six months. Actually, X-Ray was already at Camp Green Lake when Stanley arrived and—well—why give away any more of the story? But assuming that each boy remained at the camp for six months, how much dirt would X-Ray avoid removing in all by digging with a shovel that was half an inch shorter than Stanley's?

Collecting Fingerprints

Name_____

Use the following steps and help from a partner to make a set of your own fingerprints:

1. Create an "inkpad" with a sheet of notebook paper and a soft pencil. Make a large (2-inch-by-2-inch) darkened area on the paper by going over it again and again with a soft pencil (use the side of the point if doing so is easier). Make sure that the area is very dark, with multiple layers of graphite.

2. Start with your right hand and roll your thumb, from one side to the other, through the "inkpad." Lift your "inked" thumb from the "pad." Have your partner use a short strip (approximately 1 ¼ inches) of transparent tape and carefully cover the "inked" area, with "margins" of tape sticking out on either side. The tape should be applied to the fingertip in a smooth motion, with as little shifting and smudging as possible. Your partner should then carefully remove the tape, thus lifting the graphite (or a lot of it) from your thumb.

3. Your partner should then carefully affix the inked piece of tape, graphite side down, on a note card, leaving room on the card for other strips of tape for the other fingerprints from your right hand. Label card "Right Hand" and the print "Thumb." Write your name clearly on the card.

4. Continue to work with your partner to obtain prints of each of the fingers on your right hand. "Re-ink" your pad as necessary, by going over it again with your soft pencil. Label the prints in order ("Index," "Middle," "Ring," "Little") on the same note card as you obtain them.

5. When you are finished with your right hand, lift fingerprints from your left hand in the same order (thumb to little finger). Affix the tapes on the other card, label the card ("Left Hand"), and label each print. Be sure to write your name on the card.

Fingerprint Patterns

Name_____

The three basic fingerprint patterns are *loops*, *whorls*, and *arches*.

Loops

Loops are formed by ridges that enter on one side of a fingerprint, curve back, and leave on the same side. These ridges form a loop that bends toward the thumb or the little finger. A loop is identified as a *left loop* or a *right loop*.

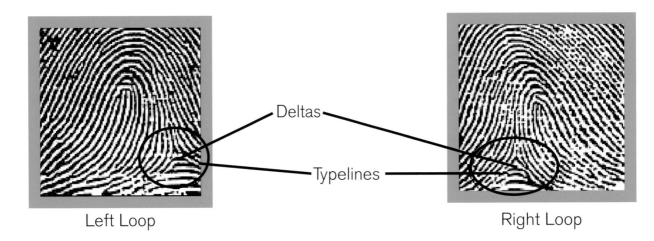

Left Loop   Right Loop

Every loop has two other important characteristics: its *typelines* and its *delta*. The typelines are ridges that enter on the opposite side from the ridges described above, which come in, curve back, and leave on one side to form the loop. The typelines start as side-by-side ridges that go close in to the loop before diverging to surround it (or to appear to surround it). Find the typelines and the point at which they diverge (in the circled area in the enlarged loop patterns pictured above). This point is known as a *delta* because it occurs where ridges on three sides make a configuration that resembles a triangle or the Greek letter Δ.

Whorl

A whorl is a complete circle in a fingerprint. Whorls are formed by ridges that enter on a side of the fingerprint, spiral inward, and end in the center. A print with a whorl typically has two deltas. Find these triangular configurations on opposite sides of the enlarged print to the right.

Whorls can be differentiated into three broad classes: plain whorls, central pocket whorls, and double loop whorls. To distinguish a plain whorl and a central pocket whorl, a fingerprint examiner uses a straightedge and makes a line connecting the deltas in the print (see the line segments drawn in the prints on the next page).

Name_____

| Plain | Central Pocket | Double Loop |

- A whorl is a *plain whorl* if the line crosses at least one complete circle in the whorl.
- A whorl is a *central pocket whorl* if the line does not cross any part of a full circle in the whorl.
- A whorl of the third type, a *double loop whorl*, is distinguished by the presence of two separate and distinct loop formations, with two *cores*. Informally, a core is the center of a pattern area; more formally, it is the point at which the innermost ridge curves back in forming the pattern in the print. Find the cores in the three prints above; the plain and central pocket whorls have one core apiece. Be sure to find both cores in the double loop whorl.

Note also that a line segment that connects the deltas in a double loop whorl cuts through the pattern area, as it does for a plain whorl. However, a double loop whorl is unlikely to be mistaken for a plain whorl. The clearly visible S-curve readily distinguishes the pattern as a double loop whorl.

Arches

Arches have ridges that enter on one side of the fingerprint, rise, and then slope back down, exiting on the opposite side of the print (see the prints below). A plain arch (see the print on the left) rises and falls fairly smoothly through the pattern area, but a *tented arch* (see the print on the right) rises up and falls down much more steeply, supported by a ridge that acts as a spine or axis for the pattern.

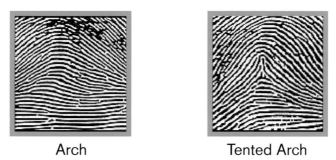

| Arch | Tented Arch |

A tented arch may appear to have a delta; however, the formal, complete definition of *delta* disqualifies the three-sided configuration in an arch from any status as a delta. By definition, a delta must be positioned so that at least one ridge that passes between it and the core of a pattern area. In a tented arch, the "pseudo-delta" is at the core of the pattern area, serving to prop it up.

Fingerprint Patterns (continued)

Name_____

1. Examine your own fingerprints. Referring to the illustrations on the preceding pages, note the features of each fingerprint. Enter each pattern type that you identify in the chart below.

My Fingerprints, Classified by Type

Right hand				
Thumb	Index	Middle	Ring	Little

Left hand				
Thumb	Index	Middle	Ring	Little

2. Count the number of arches, whorls, and loops in your set of prints.

Number of loops _____

Number of whorls _____

Number of arches _____

Fingerprinting Lab

Name_____

1. Pool your fingerprint data with your classmates' data.

2. Make a bar graph to show the frequency of loops, arches, and whorls in your class. Be sure to label your graph clearly.

3. Which pattern—arch, whorl, or loop—has the greatest frequency?

4. Rank the frequencies of the three patterns for the class.

5. Determine the percentages of loops, arches, and whorls in the data.

6. Discuss any patterns that you observe in the data.

7. Can you make any predictions about the frequencies of patterns in the general population on the basis of the data for the class? Why, or why not?

My Binary-Coded Print

Name_____

A binary classification system gives a compact way of storing data on millions of fingerprints. Such a system stores information only on whorls, which are less common than loops but more common than arches. The system pairs fingers in each set of ten prints, starting with the right hand and working from the thumb to the little finger, and then moving to the left hand and working in the same way, from the thumb to the little finger.

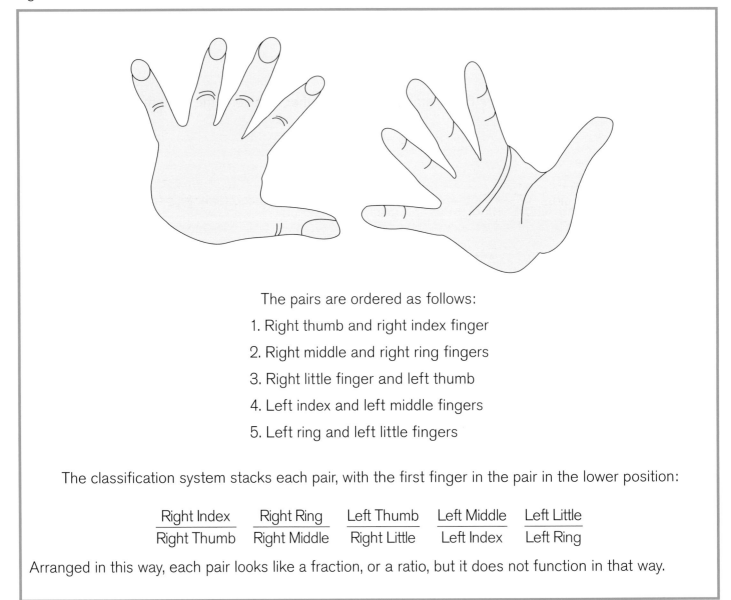

The pairs are ordered as follows:

1. Right thumb and right index finger
2. Right middle and right ring fingers
3. Right little finger and left thumb
4. Left index and left middle fingers
5. Left ring and left little fingers

The classification system stacks each pair, with the first finger in the pair in the lower position:

Right Index	Right Ring	Left Thumb	Left Middle	Left Little
Right Thumb	Right Middle	Right Little	Left Index	Left Ring

Arranged in this way, each pair looks like a fraction, or a ratio, but it does not function in that way.

A fingerprint analyst takes a set of fingerprints and gives a numerical value to each fingerprint that has a whorl. This value depends on the pair in which the whorl appears. A whorl on a finger in the first pair (right thumb and right index) receives a value of 16. (If both fingers in the pair have whorls, each receives this value.) In the second pair, any print with a whorl receives a value of 8. In the third pair, a print with a whorl gets a 4. In the fourth pair, a print with a whorl gets a 2. And in the fifth pair, a print with a whorl gets a 1.

Navigating through Mathematical Connections in Grades 6–8

Name_____

For example, if a set of prints has whorls on the right thumb, the right index finger, the left middle finger, and the left little finger, the pairs have the following numerical values:

$$\frac{16}{16} \quad \frac{0}{0} \quad \frac{0}{0} \quad \frac{2}{0} \quad \frac{1}{0}.$$

To use the binary classification system, the analyst then substitutes base-two numbers for the base-ten numbers in these expressions, as follows: $16 = 10000_2$, $8 = 1000_2$, $4 = 100_2$, $2 = 10_2$, $1 = 1_2$:

$$\frac{10000_2}{10000_2} \quad \frac{0}{0} \quad \frac{0}{0} \quad \frac{10_2}{0} \quad \frac{1}{0}.$$

The analyst then adds the top values in the stacked pairs together, and adds the bottom values together, as well:

$$\frac{10000_2+0+0+10_2+1}{10000_2+0+0+0+0} = \frac{10011_2}{10000_2}.$$

The resulting expression, $\dfrac{10011_2}{10000_2}$, is the binary code that the analyst would store for the set of prints.

1. Look again at the set of your own fingerprints that you made by following the steps on "Collecting Fingerprints." Note any fingers that contain whorls. Circle the fingers with whorls in the stacked pairs below.

Right Index	Right Ring	Left Thumb	Left Middle	Left Little
Right Thumb	Right Middle	Right Little	Left Index	Left Ring

2. Assign a value of 16 to any whorl in the first pair, an 8 to any whorl in the second pair, a 4 to any whorl in the third pair, a 2 to any whorl in the fourth pair, and a 1 to any whorl in the fifth pair. Set up your pairs below, recording a 0 for any finger without a whorl.

3. Rewrite the pairs, replacing the numbers in each with their binary equivalents ($16 = 10000_2$, $8 = 1000_2$, $4 = 100_2$, $2 = 10_2$, $1 = 1_2$).

4. Add the top numbers together, and then add the bottom numbers together. Your result should have only 1s and 0s.

This is the binary code for your set of fingerprints and should tell you exactly where whorls are present in the set.

Who Committed the Crime?

Name_____

1. A theft has occurred in your classroom! Consider the crime scene. What attributes of the thief could someone measure directly at the scene to help solve the crime?

   Your teacher (or a student in your class) has obtained direct measurements for two attributes. Record these attributes below, along with the measurements for them.

   a. _____

   b. _____

2. Do you think either of the direct measurements from (*a*) and (*b*) in step 1 might be related to another measurement that you cannot make directly but that might help you identify the thief?

   Could *both* of your direct measurements be related to this other measurement? Explain.

3. Pair each measured attribute from step 1 with the attribute that might be related to it, whose measurement is unknown.

   a. _____ and _____

   b. _____ and _____

4. Work with the other members of your group to collect data to test your conjectures about related pairs in step 3.

   a. Use the tape measures or yardsticks set up around the room to measure in each member of your group the attributes that you have identified in 3(*a*) and 3(*b*). (*Hint:* You will be making direct measurements of three attributes in each group member—the two attributes that you can measure directly in the thief and the attribute that you cannot measure directly in him or her but can measure directly in the members of the group.)

Name_____

b. Enter your data in the two "T-charts" below, using one chart for each pair of attributes that you identified in step 3 as possibly related. (*Hint:* Data on the attribute that you cannot measure directly in the thief but can measure directly in the members of your group will appear in both T-charts.)

5. Enter your group's data in the class T-charts that your teacher has set up.

6. Work with the other members of your group to make separate scatterplots on grid paper to represent the data in each class T-chart.

7. Does each class T-chart and matching scatterplot show a relationship between the measurements of the attributes? If so, describe the relationship in words and symbols.

Name_____

8. You originally measured two attributes of the thief directly. Do you believe that the measurement of either of these attributes gives you a good basis for predicting the measurement that you thought might be useful in identifying the thief but that you couldn't make directly? _____
Why, or why not?

9. Using your data, what do you think the measurement of this other attribute is for the thief?

How did you come to this conclusion?

Fishing for Data

Names _____

_____

_____

_____

_____

Your teacher has set up workstations in the classroom. At each workstation, counters (fish crackers, dried beans, etc.) serve as fish, and their container (a bowl, jar, bag, etc.) serves as the pond in which the fish live. How many fish are in the pond altogether? Call this number N. How could you make a good estimate of N without counting?

The capture-recapture method of sampling gives a way of estimating N, the total number in the population. Explore this method by working with the members of your group at one of the stations. Choose one group member to "fish" in the "pond," two members to mark and count the "fish" that are captured, and one member to make a record of all the data. The next activity sheet, "Reeling In an Estimate," will help you use these data to make a reasonable approximation of N, the number of fish in the pond.

1. **Fisherman**—Capture between 40 and 60 fish from the pond.

2. **Markers/counters**—Mark each captured fish. Use a pen to make a colored mark on both sides of each one. Count to verify that the fisherman has captured between 40 and 60 fish.

3. **Recorder**—Enter the number of fish that your group has captured and marked. Call this number M.

   $M =$ _____

4. **Fisherman**—Return the marked fish to the pond. Stir the marked and unmarked fish well in the container to simulate the mixing that would occur naturally in a pond after captured fish had been marked, counted, and released again into the water.

5. **Fisherman**—Capture another group of fish. Use the cup that is available at the workstation. Dip it into the container and fill it with fish. This catch is called a *recapture*, even though its composition is not identical to that of the original capture.

6. **Marker/counters**—Count the *total number of fish in the sample* collected in step 5. Call this number n.

   $n =$ _____

7. **Marker/counters**—Count the *number of marked fish in the sample*. Call this number m.

   $m =$ _____

Fishing for Data (continued)

Name_____

Note that capital *N* stands for the total number of individuals *in the population*, capital *M* stands for the number of marked individuals *in the population*, small *n* stands for the total number of individuals *in the sample*, and small *m* stands for the number of marked individuals *in the sample*.

8. **Recorder**—Enter your group's values for *n* and *m* in this sample (recapture 1) in the column under the numeral 1 in the table.

Recapture number	1	2	3	4	5	6	7	8	9	10
Total number of fish in the recapture (*n*)										
Number of marked fish in the recapture (*m*)										

9. **Fisherman**—Again return the fish to the pond. Stir the returned sample well once again, to simulate the natural mixing of fish in the pond.

10. **Fisherman, markers/counters, and recorder**—Repeat steps 5–9 *nine more times*, to gather and record data for a total of ten samples.

Reeling In an Estimate

Name_____

Now that you have gathered data on the fish in your pond by using the capture-recapture method of sampling, you're set to estimate N, the total number of fish in your pond.

For convenience, transfer your group's data from the activity sheet "Fishing for Data" to this sheet. (Refer to steps 3 and 8 on "Fishing for Data.")

$M =$ _____

Recapture number	1	2	3	4	5	6	7	8	9	10
Total number of fish in the recapture (n)										
Number of marked fish in the recapture (m)										

Take the following steps to estimate N:

1. Find the average value of n. _____

2. Find the average value of m. _____

3. N stands for the total number of fish in the pond. The value of N is unknown; it is what you are interested in estimating. M stands for the total number of fish that you originally marked and returned to the pond. Then, with all the fish sufficiently mixed, you began recapturing fish. The value of n that you found in step 1 above represents the average number of fish in a recaptured sample. The value of m that you found in step 2 represents the average number of marked fish in a recaptured sample. Consider the following proportional relationship:

$$\frac{M}{N} = \frac{m}{n}.$$

Do you think it is reasonable to suppose that the ratios $\dfrac{M}{N}$ and $\dfrac{m}{n}$ would be equal? _____
Explain your thinking.

Name_____

4. C. G. J. Petersen used the capture-recapture sampling technique in 1896 to estimate the population of harvestable fish in Danish waters. F. C. Lincoln used it in 1930 to estimate waterfowl abundance in U.S. flyways. The technique is sometimes called the Lincoln-Petersen method. Assuming that the ratios $\frac{M}{N}$ and $\frac{m}{n}$ are equal, solving the equation $\frac{M}{N} = \frac{m}{n}$ for N gives an estimate of N that is known as the *Lincoln index*:

$$N = \frac{nM}{m}.$$

Find the Lincoln index as an estimate of your population of fish in the pond.

5. In 1951, D. G. Chapman showed that when the size of the sample is small, the estimate of the population produced by the Lincoln index is *biased*. In statistics, data that are biased are prone to, or likely to include, error. Chapman suggested that the Lincoln index gives an overestimate of the population under consideration. He modified the equation used in the Lincoln index to adjust and reduce the result. Chapman added a "correcting factor" (+ 1) to each quantity in the equation:

$$\frac{M+1}{N+1} = \frac{m+1}{n+1};$$

$$N+1 = \frac{(n+1)(M+1)}{m+1};$$

$$N = \frac{(n+1)(M+1)}{m+1} - 1 = N_C.$$

This modification of the Lincoln index is called the *Chapman population estimate*, often denoted as N_C. Calculate the Chapman population estimate of the fish in the pond.

$$N_C = \frac{(n+1)(M+1)}{m+1} - 1 =$$

6. Now make an actual count of the fish in the pond. (This is something that ecologists and wildlife biologists obviously cannot do, but you can make this count as a check of your estimates.)

$N_{actual} =$

Name_____

7. How close were your estimates to the actual *N*? You can find the percentage difference between each of your estimates and the actual population by using the following formula:

$$\% \text{ difference} = \frac{(\text{larger number}) - (\text{smaller number})}{\text{average of the two numbers}} \times 100$$

Calculate the difference for both the Lincoln index and the Chapman population estimate that you obtained for your population of fish in the pond.

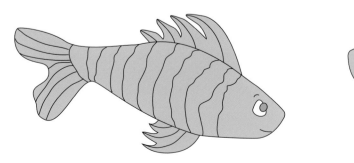

Solutions for the Blackline Masters

Solutions for "Pyramid Scheme?"

Ritzville Experiments—Part 1

1. *a.* Students' definitions will vary but should include the information that a pyramid is a solid whose base is a polygon and whose other faces are triangles that have a common vertex.

   b. Students should conclude that the term *pyramid* is not correct for the shape of the pile of rice, since its base would be circular rather than polygonal (it would have no sides), and its lateral surface would have no triangular faces.

   c. The students should expect a very large pile of wheat to be shaped like a cone.

2. *a* and *b.* Check to be sure that in the experiment the students are pouring the rice *slowly* onto the paper towel.

   c. The students' drawings from a vantage point directly above the rice should show an oval or circle.

   d. The students' side views of their piles of rice will probably show a fairly flat mound.

3. *a.* The students' drawings from a vantage point directly above the rice should show an oval or circle that is larger than the one that they drew in 2(*c*).

   b. The students' side views of their piles of rice should show a mound that is somewhat larger and slightly less flat than the one that they drew in 2(*d*).

4. *a.* The students' drawings from a vantage point directly above the rice should show an oval or circle that is larger than the one that they drew in 3(*a*).

   b. The students' side views of their piles of rice should show a mound that is somewhat larger than the one that they drew in 3(*b*) and is starting to come to a point.

5. The students should see that their piles of rice are beginning to be cone shaped. Their statements will differ about whether or not this was the shape that they expected, and why.

Solutions for "Ritzville Reflections"

Ritzville Experiments—Part 2

1. Although the students may not have the vocabulary to express the idea in this way, they should recognize that to find the amount of vinyl that was necessary to cover their pile of wheat, they would need to find the lateral surface area of the cone formed by the wheat.

2. The students should recognize that to find the amount of wheat in their stack, they would need to find the volume of the cone of wheat.

Solutions for "Sizing Up a Cylinder"

Ritzville Experiments—Part 3

1. Students' answers will vary.

2. Making the shortest cut possible guarantees that the resulting net will be rectangular.

3. The net that the students make of the lateral surface of the cylinder is rectangular. (If their cut spiraled down the cylinder's lateral surface, the resulting net would be a parallelogram instead of a rectangle.)

4–7. Answers and work will vary, but students should gradually develop a sense of how large the circular bases need to be in relation to the net of the lateral surface of a particular cylinder, and where they should place the circles for the bases. They should see that the circumference of each base is equal to the length of the top or bottom edge of the rectangular net of the lateral surface, and they should understand that they can place one circle anywhere along the top edge of the rectangle, and the other circle anywhere along the bottom edge, to complete the net of the cylinder. (See the discussion on p. 18.)

Side View

Lateral Surface

Base

Solutions for "Conic Considerations"

Ritzville Experiments—Part 4

1. *a* and *b*. Students' answers will vary. Some may suppose that the net of a cone without a base will be an isosceles triangle. Others may suppose that it will be an isosceles triangle with a semicircle on its base. Still others may conjecture that the shape of the net of a cone without a base is part of a circular region—a *sector* of a circle.

2. Making the shortest cut possible guarantees that the length of a cut edge will be equal to the slant height of the cone.

3. Students' answers will vary.

4–7. Answers and work will vary, but the process that the students go through should show them that the lateral surface of a cone is part of a circular region, and the base is circular. The students should gradually develop a sense of how large the circular base needs to be in relation to the curved edge of the net of the lateral surface of a particular cone and where they should place the circle for the base. They should see that the circumference of the base is equal to the length of the curved edge of the net of the lateral surface, and they should understand that they can place the circle anywhere along the curved edge to complete the net of the cylinder. (See the discussion in the text on p. 19.)

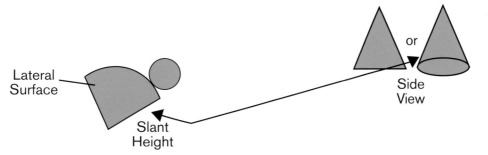

Lateral Surface

Slant Height

Side View

or

The students should also become aware that the slant height of the cone is one of the straight edges of the lateral surface.

Solutions for "Completing the Circle"

Ritzville Experiments—Part 5

1–3. Guide the students through the process of measuring one of their assigned angles as a central angle of one of the disks, cutting out the resulting sector, and labeling it, as well as the sector that remains. See the discussion on page 21 for two methods of determining the center of the disk.

4. As the students compare the cut sectors to the whole, uncut disk, their conjectures may vary. Many may suppose, correctly, that knowing the central angles of the sectors can help them determine the fraction of the circumference of the whole circle that the circumference of the sector represents.

5–6. The students should work carefully with string and grid paper to obtain useful measurements of the circumferences and areas of their sectors.

7. *a* and *b*. Students' calculations of the circumference and area of the uncut disk will depend on the size of the disk.

8–11. If the students have worked carefully and obtained reasonably accurate results, the fractions that they write for the ratios $\dfrac{C_{sector}}{C_{circle}}$ and $\dfrac{A_{sector}}{A_{circle}}$ should lead them to suspect that the ratios are equal.

Solutions for "Developing the Data"

Ritzville Experiments—Part 6

1 and 2. Students' values in columns 3 and 5 will vary, depending on the sizes of their disks and the accuracy of their measurements. A partially completed chart appears on the opposite page. It shows experimental results for the areas of sectors with a radius of 12 cm, and it uses 3.14 as an approximation for π. Thus, the area of the circle is approximately 452.2 cm^2.

3. Using their experimental data, the students should observe that the ratios are close to equal.

4. Students' calculations of the measurements of the circumferences and areas of their sectors will vary, depending on the size of their disks and the approximation that they use for π.

5. Students' answers will vary.

6. Be sure that your students align the radii of each sector *with no overlap* in making their cones.

(1) Angle measurement (degrees)	(2) Fraction of a circle	(3) Circumference of the sector (C_{sector}) in the experiment (cm)	(4) Ratio $\dfrac{C_{sector}}{C_{circle}}$	(5) Area of the sector (A_{sector}) in the experiment (cm²)	(6) Ratio $\dfrac{A_{sector}}{A_{circle}}$
30°	$\dfrac{1}{12} = 0.083$			38	$\dfrac{38}{452.2} = 0.084$
45°	$\dfrac{1}{8} = 0.125$			57	$\dfrac{57}{452.2} = 0.126$
60°	$\dfrac{1}{6} = 0.167$			76	$\dfrac{76}{452.2} = 0.168$
90°	$\dfrac{1}{4} = 0.25$			114	$\dfrac{114}{452.2} = 0.252$
120°	$\dfrac{1}{3} = 0.333$			152	$\dfrac{152}{452.2} = 0.336$
135°	$\dfrac{3}{8} = 0.375$			171	$\dfrac{171}{452.2} = 0.378$
150°	$\dfrac{5}{12} = 0.417$			190	$\dfrac{190}{452.2} = 0.42$
180°	$\dfrac{1}{2} = 0.5$			229	$\dfrac{229}{452.2} = 0.506$
210°	$\dfrac{7}{12} = 0.583$			266	$\dfrac{266}{452.2} = 0.588$
225°	$\dfrac{5}{8} = 0.625$			286	$\dfrac{286}{452.2} = 0.632$
240°	$\dfrac{2}{3} = 0.667$			305	$\dfrac{305}{452.2} = 0.674$
270°	$\dfrac{3}{4} = 0.75$			343	$\dfrac{343}{452.2} = 0.759$
300°	$\dfrac{5}{6} = 0.833$			381	$\dfrac{381}{452.2} = 0.843$
315°	$\dfrac{7}{8} = 0.875$			400	$\dfrac{400}{452.2} = 0.885$
330°	$\dfrac{11}{12} = 0.917$			419	$\dfrac{419}{452.2} = 0.927$

Solutions for "Coming to the Surface"

Ritzville Experiments—Part 7

1–3. Below is a sketch of the sector representing the lateral surface of the students' cone-shaped stack of wheat in Ritzville, Washington. The circumference of the sector (C_{sector}, which is the circumference of the base of the conical stack) is 482 feet, and the slant height (s) of the cone is 91 feet. The students must find the area of the sector (A_{sector}), which is shown as a missing value in the sketch. The sketch also shows as a missing value the circumference of the whole circle (C_{circle}) of which the sector is a part.

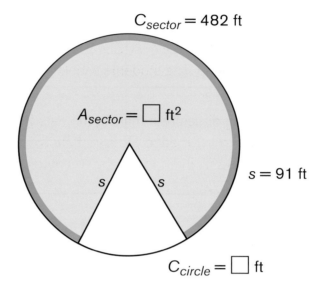

$C_{sector} = 482$ ft

$A_{sector} = \square$ ft^2

$s = 91$ ft

$C_{circle} = \square$ ft

Such a sketch, even if it does not represent the area or central angle of the sector accurately, can help students organize information and see what they are working to find.

4. The students use the formula $C \approx 2\pi r$ to find the circumference of the circle of which the sector is a part. They should not use an approximation for π in the calculation:

$$C_{circle} \approx 2\pi(91) \approx 182\pi \text{ ft.}$$

5. The students use the formula $A = \pi r^2$ to find the area of the circle of which the sector is a part. Again, they should not use an approximation for π in the calculation:

$$A_{circle} \approx \pi(91^2) \approx 8281\pi \text{ ft}^2.$$

6. Because $\dfrac{C_{sector}}{C_{circle}} = \dfrac{A_{sector}}{A_{circle}}$, as the students have discovered, $\dfrac{C_{sector}}{C_{circle}} \cdot A_{circle} = A_{sector}$. By substituting, the students get $\dfrac{482}{182\pi} \cdot 8281\pi \approx 21{,}900 \text{ ft}^2$.

Solutions for "Volumes Yet to Learn!"

Ritzville Experiments—Part 8

1. This time the students would need to measure the volume of their stack.

2. The measurement would be in cubic units because it would measure the space that the stack occupies in three dimensions.

Solutions for "Can You Be More Precise?"

Ritzville Experiments—Part 9

1–3. Students can work with their cones from part 5 ("Completing the Circle"). The sectors of their cones will represent different fractions of a circle. The students should recognize that they will be using cubic units to measure the volume of their cones.

4. Guide the students if they are having difficulty in making the nets for a cube that is 2 centimeters on an edge and a cube that is 1 centimeter on an edge. Be sure that the students tape their "boxes" together carefully without gaps or overlaps and fill them to the top with rice.

5. *a.* The students should report that the cube that is 1 cm on an edge holds 1 cubic centimeter (1 cm^3) of rice.

   b. The students should report that the cube that is 2 cm on an edge holds 8 cubic centimeters (8 cm^3) of rice.

6. *a.* When the students pour the rice from the cube that is 1 cm on an edge into a small (10 mL) graduated cylinder, they should see that it is equal to 1 mL. A cubic centimeter of rice occupies the same amount of space as a milliliter of rice. Usually small amounts of dry quantities are measured in cubic centimeters, and small amounts of liquid are measured in milliliters. However, the students will be measuring the rice in milliliters, because that is how the graduated cylinders are calibrated, but they will be converting each milliliter to a cubic centimeter in order to compare their measurements with other measurements.

   b. No, this measurement is not in the units that the students used before to report the measurement. It is in milliliters instead of cubic centimeters.

   c and *d.* The students should see that 1 cm^3 = 1 mL.

7. *a.* When the students pour the rice from the cube that is 2 cm on an edge into a small graduated cylinder, they should see that is equal to 8 mL.

   b and *c.* The students should see that 8 mL is equal to 8 cm^3, the measurement that they reported earlier.

8–13. Guide the students as they use plastic cubes (2 cm on an edge and 1 cm on an edge) and rice poured directly into their cones to estimate the volume of rice that each cone will hold. Be sure that the students understand the data that they enter into the chart. The students should see that their estimates are becoming larger and more precise as they use smaller and smaller units to approximate the volume of each cone. A sample chart appears at the top of the next page for cones that students made from two circles with a radius of 7 cm (that is, cone A and cone B are not complements).

	Fraction of the circle	Number (N) of cubes (2×2×2 cm³) needed to fill cone	Amount of rice in N cubes (cm³)	Number (M) of cubes (1×1×1 cm³) needed to fill cone	Amount of rice in M cubes (cm³)	Amount of rice needed to fill cone directly (cm³)
Cone A	$\frac{5}{8}$	5	40	72	72	115
Cone B	$\frac{11}{12}$	6	48	96	96	120

Solutions for "Turning Up the Volume"

Ritzville Experiments—Part 10

The sample spreadsheet below and graph at the top of the next page were created by students to represent their data on cones made from sectors cut from a circle with a radius of 7 cm. Note that (1) the spreadsheet shows only the data obtained by measuring with "large blocks" (2 cm on an edge), (2) the students' graph shows (in green) a plot of the volume of the cone as a function of the central angle of the sector from which it was formed, and (3) these students made cones by removing central angles that differ from those identified for the activity.

Volume of Cones with base readius of 7 cm				
cone	Angle Removed (degrees)	Volume (cc)	Unit of Measure	Angle Remaining (degrees)
1	15	32	Large Blocks	345
2	30	40	Large Blocks	330
3	45	56	Large Blocks	315
4	50	64	Large Blocks	310
5	56	64	Large Blocks	304
6	60	64	Large Blocks	300
7	62	72	Large Blocks	298
8	65	56	Large Blocks	295
9	70	56	Large Blocks	290
10	88	48	Large Blocks	272
11	100	56	Large Blocks	260
12	110	48	Large Blocks	250
13	118	48	Large Blocks	242
14	135	48	Large Blocks	225

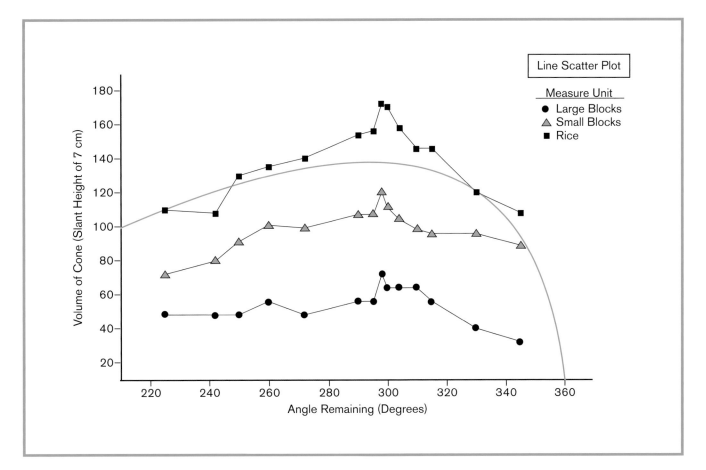

1. *a–c.* Your students' compiled data show measurements of the volume of each cone made in the three ways that part 9 of Ritzville Experiments calls for—with cubes that are 2 centimeters on an edge, with cubes that are 1 centimeter on an edge, and by pouring rice into the cones directly. The students then graph the results, showing each set of measurements in a different color. They put the fraction of the circle on the horizontal axis and the volume on the vertical axis, labeling it with the correct units (cm^3).

   d. Your students should connect the dots for each type of measurement, as the students have done in the sample graph above, because the measurement of the central angle of a circle is continuous. They should understand that they don't need to measure the angles only in a whole number of degrees. Between any two whole-numbered measurements, they could find measurements for as many more angles as they want.

2. *a.* The students should understand that their measurements on the graphs are not the same because they used different-sized units to measure. They should also see that measuring by pouring rice directly into the cones gives the most precise measurements. The rice fills more of the space inside the cones, but the cubes have gaps between them, so the measurements that they give leave out part of the volume.

   b. Students' responses will vary.

3. *a.* The cone with the largest volume is formed from a sector whose area represents approximately $\frac{5}{6}$ of the whole circle.

   b. Someone removed an angle of approximately 60° to make the sector for this cone.

   c. A central angle of approximately 300° remained.

4. Students' responses and explanations will vary.

As suggested in the extensions proposed text (see p. 35), if you would like to give your students a real-world context in which they might want to maximize the volume of a cone, consider sharing with them the following scenario: "Suppose that we are going to have a school fair, and we are going to be responsible for the snow-cone booth. We have cut out heavy paper circles that we are going to use to make cones to hold flavored crushed ice. We want all the cones to be same size and to hold as much flavored ice as possible. So each cone should be the cone of greatest volume that we can make from our circle."

Solutions for "A Second Look at Cylinders"

Ritzville Experiments—Part 11

1. *a* and *b*. Students' responses will vary. Some may readily understand that the formula for the volume of a cylinder is $V_{cylinder} = \pi r^2 h$. Others may need some guidance to make sense of the formula. A close comparison of it with the formula for the volume of a rectangular prism ($V = l \times w \times h$) may help the students understand the new formula.

2. *a–d*. Students' responses will vary. Be sure that your students understand what they are doing when they use the familiar formula $C = 2\pi r$ to determine the radius of the base of their cone and when they use the Pythagorean theorem to determine its height.

3. *a–c*. Observe your students as they calculate the volume of the cylinder that has the same radius and height as their cone. Be sure that they then compare to this measurement the measurement that they obtained earlier for the volume of the cone by pouring rice directly into it: $\dfrac{V_{cone}}{V_{cylinder}}$. The ratio should be close to $\dfrac{1}{3}$.

4–5. The students' pooling of their data and organizing them in the chart should give them ratios that are similar to one another and that are consistently close to the fraction $\dfrac{1}{3}$. They may conjecture that the formula for the volume of a cone is $\dfrac{1}{3} \pi r^2 h$.

Solutions for "A Value for the Volume"

Ritzville Experiments—Part 12

1. The students should understand that they will be measuring the volume of wheat in their stack in cubic feet (ft³).

2. *a*. Using $C = 2\pi r$ with C equal to 482 feet and solving for r, the students will obtain

$$482 \approx 2\pi r$$

$$r \approx \frac{241}{\pi} \text{ft}$$

$$r \approx 77 \text{ ft.}$$

b. Using the Pythagorean theorem to obtain h, the height of the conical stack of wheat, gives

$$h^2 + (77)^2 \approx (91)^2$$
$$h^2 \approx (91)^2 - (77)^2$$
$$h^2 \approx 8281 - 5929$$
$$h \approx \sqrt{2352}$$
$$h \approx 48 \text{ ft.}$$

3. *a–c.* Substituting for r and h in the formula for the volume of a cone gives

$$V_{cone} = \frac{1}{3}\pi r^2 h$$
$$\approx \frac{1}{3}\left(\frac{22}{7}\right)(77)^2(48)$$
$$\approx \frac{22}{21}(5929)(48)$$
$$\approx 298{,}000 \text{ ft}^3.$$

4. Using the equivalence 1 bu ≈ 1.25 ft³, the students should find that their stack contains approximately 238,000 bushels of wheat.

Solutions for "Sizing the Silhouette"

Solutions are discussed in the text (see pp. 45–46); the perimeter of the silhouette is about 104 linear grid units, and its area is about 345 square units. A possible breakdown of the area and perimeter of half of the silhouette (divided by the shuttle's line of symmetry) is shown at the right. Circled numbers indicate areas in square units for the regions in which they appear.

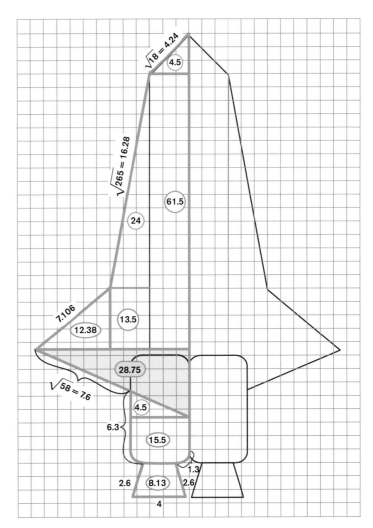

Solutions for "Marvels of Flight"

The NASA CONNECT activity "Geometry and Algebra: The Future Flight Equation" has its own activity pages (consequently, there are no blackline masters in the appendix of this book). A chart from the activity appears at the right, with data entered by students in one classroom. Photocopying may slightly alter sizes of the templates for the wings, resulting in variations in measurements.

Data Chart

	Wing Area (cm²)	Wing Span (cm)	Root Chord (cm)	Tip Chord (cm)	Average Chord (cm)	Aspect Ratio
Oblique Wing	153 cm²	28 cm	7 cm	—	3.5 cm	8
Delta Wing	165 cm²	22 cm	15		7.5 cm	2.9
Straight Wing	144 cm²	24 cm	8 cm	4 cm	6 cm	4
Swept-Back Wing	111 cm²	19 cm	8 cm	4 cm	6 cm	3.1

The tables below show results from one class for the four wing types. Data will of course vary from group to group. *Note:* Ratings of glide and speed are evaluated observationally on a scale of 1 to 5; the "overall" rating is an average of the observational glide and speed ratings.

Oblique Wing	Distance (cm)	Glide Rating (1–5)	Speed Rating (1–5)	Overall
Trial 1	202	3	2	2.5
Trial 2	303	2	4	3
Trial 3	381	4	3	3.5
Trial 4	301	5	3	4
Trial 5	293	4	3	3.5
Average	**296**	**3.6**	**3**	**3.3**

Delta Wing	Distance (cm)	Glide Rating (1–5)	Speed Rating (1–5)	Overall
Trial 1	300	3	4	3.5
Trial 2	370	3	4	3.5
Trial 3	690	5	5	5
Trial 4	503	4	5	4.5
Trial 5	240	5	5	5
Average	**420**	**4**	**4.6**	**4.3**

Straight Wing	Distance (cm)	Glide Rating (1–5)	Speed Rating (1–5)	Overall
Trial 1	181	5	3	4
Trial 2	257	5	4	4.5
Trial 3	232	5	3	4
Trial 4	160	2	3	2.5
Trial 5	196	3	4	3.5
Average	**205**	**4**	**3.4**	**3.7**

Swept-Back Wing	Distance (cm)	Glide Rating (1–5)	Speed Rating (1–5)	Overall
Trial 1	810	5	5	5
Trial 2	770	5	5	5
Trial 3	795	5	5	5
Trial 4	692	4	4	4
Trial 5	407	5	5	5
Average	**695**	**4.8**	**4.8**	**4.8**

Solutions for "Dinosaur Scaling"

1. Students' measurements will vary. The measurements below come from the data from one class. All measurements are in centimeters.

Attribute	Measurement in Scale Drawing (cm)	Measurement in Real Life (cm)	Attribute	Measurement in Scale Drawing (cm)	Measurement in Real Life (cm)
Total Length	16	224	Length of Head	1.	14
Hip Height	4.	56	Width of Head	0.5	7
Length of Body	4.2	58.8	Length of Humerus	1.1	15.4
Depth of Body	1.5	21	Diameter of Humerus	0.3	4.2
Length of Femur	1.8	25.2	Length of Radius	1.2	16.8
Diameter of Femur	0.5	7	Diameter of Radius	0.2	2.8
Length of Tibia	1.2	16.8	Length of Tail	6.5	91
Diameter of Tibia	0.2	2.8	Tail Diameter at Body	0.3	4.2

2. *a.* The elastic scale based on the 1 : 14 scale that the students used is 1 : $(14)^{\frac{3}{2}}$ or approximately 1 : 52.4.

   b. Applying elastic scaling to the measurements that the students recorded above for the diameters of the weight-bearing bones gives the following "real-life" diameters:

   • Femur: 0.5 • 52.4 ≈ 26.2 cm
   • Tibia: 0.2 • 52.4 ≈ 10.5 cm
   • Humerus: 0.3 • 52.4 ≈ 15.7 cm
   • Radius: 0.2 • 52.4 ≈ 10.5 cm
   • Tail: 0.3 • 52.4 ≈ 15.7 cm

c. The students should reason that support bones need to be thicker than other bones because they must be strong enough to hold up an animal. The diameters determined for these bones by using an elastic scale are greater than diameters determined by using a more general scale for length. The diameters that result from elastic scaling give a more accurate representation of the thickness of the weight-bearing bones.

Solutions for "Digging *Holes*"

1. Students' responses will vary. To help your students think about the difference in terms of cubic units, show them a cubic inch and a cubic foot.

2. A circle with a diameter of 5 inches has an area of $\pi(2.5)^2 = \pi (6.25) \approx 19.63$ square inches. A circle with a diameter of 4.5 inches has an area of $\pi(2.25)^2 \approx \pi (5.06) \approx 15.89$ square inches. The difference is approximately 3.7 square inches.

3. Students' responses will vary. Some students might note that they had to find half of the diameter before using the formula for the area of a circle ($A = \pi r^2$). Others might observe that the difference was greater than they thought it would be. Students might also compare their findings to the circles they drew, noting that they look about the same size but are not.

4. Students' responses will vary.

5. Stanley's hole is 5 feet deep and 5 feet across. The radius of its circular base is thus 2.5 feet. The volume of the cylindrical hole is $\pi r^2 h$. Substituting gives

$$\pi(2.5)^2 (5) = \pi(31.25) \approx 98.1 \text{ ft}^3,$$

using 3.14 for π and rounding to the nearest tenth. In cubic inches, the volume of Stanley's hole is

$$\pi(30)^2 (60) = \pi (54000) \approx 169,560 \text{ in}^3.$$

By contrast, X-Ray's hole is 4 feet 11.5 inches deep and 4 feet 11.5 inches across. Because 11.5 inches is approximately 0.96 feet, the radius of the circular base is about $4.96 \div 2$, or 2.48, feet. Thus, in cubic feet, the volume of X-Ray's hole is

$$\pi(2.48)^2 (4.96) \approx \pi(30.5) \approx 95.79 \text{ ft}^3.$$

The radius in inches of X-Ray's hole is $59.5 \div 2$, or 29.75, inches. The volume of the hole in cubic inches is thus

$$\pi(29.75)^2(59.5) \approx \pi(52661.22) \approx 165,356 \text{ in}^3.$$

Note that the volumes in cubic feet and cubic inches computed above for Stanley's and X-Ray's holes contain round-off error. Consequently, multiplying the measurements in cubic feet by 1728 does not yield the measurements obtained for the holes in cubic inches.

6. Working with the computations in cubic inches yields the following difference between the volume of Stanley's hole and the volume of X-Ray's hole:

$$169,560 - 165,356 = 4,204 \text{ in}^3;$$

$$4,204 \div 1728 \approx 2.43 \text{ ft}^3.$$

7. Solutions will vary.

8. Students' responses will vary.

9. Students' responses will vary.

Solutions for "Getting the *Holes* Picture"

1. Students' numbers in the tables below may vary as a result of round-off error in their calculations.

Stanley

Number of Weeks	Dirt Removed (ft³)
1	687
2	1374
3	2061
4	2748
5	3435

X-Ray

Number of Weeks	Dirt Removed (ft³)
1	670
2	1340
3	2010
4	2680
5	3350

2. *a.* Students' explanations will vary.

   b. Let y_S stand for the dirt removed by Stanley, and let x stand for the number of weeks in which Stanley has dug holes. Then $y_S \approx 687x$ is a rule for the amount of dirt that Stanley would have removed by the end of any given week x.

   c. Let y_R stand for the dirt removed by X-Ray, and let x stand for the number of weeks in which X-Ray has dug holes. The $y_R \approx 670x$ is a rule for the amount of dirt that X-Ray would have removed by the end of any given week x.

3. Let y_D stand for the difference in the dirt that the boys would have removed in a given number of weeks (x) at Camp Green Lake. A rule for the difference is $y_D \approx 17x$. (The difference for one day is approximately 2.4 cubic feet, so the difference for a week is $2.4 \times 7 = 16.8 \approx 17$, and the cumulative difference at the end of any given week x is $17x$.

4. If Stanley and X-Ray both dug holes for six months, X-Ray would dig approximately 442 cubic feet less than Stanley. Because 6 months $\approx$ 26 weeks, students can simply use their rule for the difference, $y_D \approx 17x$:

$$y_D \approx (17)(26) \approx 442 \text{ ft}^3.$$

Alternatively, they can apply the rules for the amounts of dirt removed by Stanley and X-Ray and find the difference:

$$687 \cdot 26 \approx 17{,}862 \text{ ft}^3 \text{ removed by Stanley}$$
$$670 \cdot 26 \approx 17{,}420 \text{ ft}^3 \text{ removed by X-Ray}$$
$$17{,}862 - 17{,}420 = 442 \text{ ft}^3$$

X-Ray would have removed approximately 442 cubic feet less dirt from his holes over six months than Stanley would have removed from his over the same period of time. The difference is sizeable.

Solutions for "Collecting Fingerprints" and "Fingerprint Patterns"

Observe the students closely as they work with their partners to follow the steps on the blackline master and obtain a set of their own fingerprints. Be sure that students are managing to lift legible prints with graphite and tape. Guide them in arranging the prints on the 4-by-6-inch cards if necessary.

Solutions for "Fingerprinting Lab"

Data will vary from class to class. Percentages for one class were as follows: loops—61%; whorls—26%; arches—13%. The students should conclude that their class data set is too small to use to make any meaningful predictions about frequencies of patterns in the general population.

Solutions for "My Binary-Coded Print"

Students' responses will vary.

Solutions for "Who Committed the Crime?"

1. Someone could measure the length of the thief's shoe and his or her stride length.

2. Many students will suggest that the measurements from step 1 may be related to height. If not, guide them to this idea.

3. The students will be investigating the relationships between shoe length and height and stride length and height.

4. Students' data (measurements of their shoe lengths, stride lengths, and heights) will vary.

5. Students' data in the class T-charts will vary.

6. Be sure that students' scatterplots show height on the y-axis and either shoe length or stride length on the x-axis.

7. Students' responses will vary. Students in most classrooms have found linear trends in at least one of the scatterplots. Classes in which students' heights vary significantly are more likely to have an identifiable linear trend in the data.

8. Responses will vary. Students might write that as the shoe length or stride length increases, the height also increases. They might discuss the clustering of the data points, the quantity of data collected, and the spread of the data.

9. Responses will vary. Students should use either the equation they created or the scatterplot to select a height.

Solutions for "Fishing for Data"

Observe the students as they work at the stations to gather their capture-recapture samples. If they are using fish crackers as counters, tell them to stir the crackers carefully when they mix them so that the crackers do not break.

Solutions for "Reeling in an Estimate"

The following notes and suggestions come from a teacher whose students completed the activity How Many Fish in the Pond?

Below are data from two simulations in my classroom to give an idea of the results that students might obtain when they perform this experiment. I am assuming that there are 300 fish in the pond (that is, 300 crackers in the container).

First, the students "capture" between 40 and 60 fish and mark them. Then they put these fish back into the pond and mix them up really well. Next, they capture a cupful of fish and count the number captured (n) and the number of these that are marked (m).

Experiment 1 $M = 43$			Experiment 2 $M = 46$		
Trial Number	Number of Fish Caught (n)	Number of Marked Fish (m)	Trial Number	Number of Fish Caught (n)	Number of Marked Fish (m)
1	21	0	1	26	1
2	26	1	2	23	2
3	29	4	3	29	3
4	26	2	4	29	1
5	20	1	5	32	3
6	26	1	6	31	2
7	29	4	7	26	1
8	29	2	8	33	1
9	20	2	9	29	0
10	28	1	10	25	1

Next, the students must find the averages of the n's and m's to use in getting two population estimates—the Lincoln index and the Chapman population estimate:

Experiment 1 $M = 43$	Experiment 2 $M = 46$
$\bar{n} = \dfrac{n_1 + n_2 \ldots + n_{10}}{10} = 25.4$ $\bar{m} = \dfrac{m_1 + m_2 \ldots + m_{10}}{10} = 1.8$	$\bar{n} = \dfrac{n_1 + n_2 \ldots + n_{10}}{10} = 28.3$ $\bar{m} = \dfrac{m_1 + m_2 \ldots + m_{10}}{10} = 1.5$
Lincoln index: $N = \dfrac{\bar{n}M}{\bar{m}} \approx 607$	Lincoln index: $N = \dfrac{\bar{n}M}{\bar{m}} \approx 868$
Chapman population estimate: $N_C = \dfrac{(\bar{n}+1)(M+1)}{(\bar{m}+1)} - 1 \approx 414$	Chapman population estimate: $N_C = \dfrac{(\bar{n}+1)(M+1)}{(\bar{m}+1)} - 1 \approx 550$

The estimates based on my students' data are not really close to the actual population. However, the Chapman population estimate gives a much better count in these cases. Below are several questions that I have raised with my students:

• "Why do these techniques not give us better estimates of the actual population size?" (The size of the initial sample was too small.)

• "Why is the Chapman estimate a better measure of population size in our experiments?" (The Chapman estimate adjusts the numbers to make up for the smallness of the initial sample size in the experiments.)

If there had been time to extend the exercise, the students could have taken an initial sample of between 80 and 100 fish. Then they could have taken a recapture sample of almost the same size and made estimates on the basis of their new data.